HANDBOOK
for the
EMERGING
WOMAN

HANDBOOK
for the
EMERGING
WOMAN

Mary Elizabeth Marlow

HAMPTON ROADS
PUBLISHING COMPANY, INC.

For information write:

Hampton Roads Publishing Company, Inc.
891 Norfolk Square
Norfolk, VA 23502

Or call: (804)459-2453
FAX: (804)455-8907

If you are unable to order this book from your local
bookseller, you may order directly from the publisher.
Quantity discounts for organizations are available.
Call 1-800-766-8009, toll-free.

ISBN 1-878901-78-8

Printed on acid-free paper in the United States of America

To the women who have
opened their hearts
and shared deeply
of their grief and wounds,
their joys and triumphs.
All of them
have taught me well
about the profound,
endless transformative power
of women.

Contents

The Bitch is that part of us that is connected to our feelings of powerlessness. We nag, grouch, whine, withdraw, shout, or shut down because we don't feel we have other options. Once we learn how to clearly identify and name our Bitch, we are able to move decisively to our real power and true identity.

The Dragon Fight is the struggle we have with ourselves when we reject and rebel against our parents or strive to emulate them. Learning to identify both the obvious and the hidden "Dragons" allows us to understand our female-male polarity and our relationship patterns.

Betrayal is the death of trust. It is important to know how we set ourselves up for betrayal experiences, what we can learn from them (don't waste a good betrayal!) and how we can move beyond betrayal.

The ability to transform life's experiences is not new. It has been known in many ancient cultures, including the Native American. They have a respect and understanding of the feminine power of nature. As women, we too can tap into the transformational energy of these four elements (fire, earth, air, and water).

The pantheon of Greek goddesses reflects the diversity and complexity within women and provides us with a new way of looking at ourselves from a perspective which is thoroughly feminine. As we awaken and search for wholeness, the goddesses return to help us in our journey.

Contents

Preface

To emerge as a woman is an exquisite dance. We stretch. We reach out, we express, we move, sometimes boldly, sometimes timidly, sometimes gracefully, sometimes awkwardly. We take a step forward; we take a step backwards. And then, unsure, we listen in stillness to sense our rhythm once more, to know when to, whether to, or even if we should dance. We leap up with joy. We bend over in pain. Yet we still dance. In time, we embrace it all. We dance on it all.

This Handbook is the dance of women opening to the full depth, power, and potency of being women. It is women moving with and through their weaknesses, their strengths, their challenges, their defeats, their victories, and their triumphs. It is women knowing and accepting themselves. It is women discovering the joy of being a woman.

The stories are of women who are old, young, rich, poor, white, black, educated, uneducated, sick, well, American, European. They are real stories of real women. Each chapter relates to an essential step, an initiation, through which every woman moves in her emerging process. These steps are graduated and build on the one before. Each chapter presents at least one or more experiential process to measure and validate your own progress. Your chronology may be slightly different than the one suggested in the Handbook, but you will, no doubt, identify with the challenges inherent in the different initiations.

Your journey through the *Handbook* can be a private one or a shared experience. The *Handbook* is designed so that it can be used individually, with close friends, or in a support group.

It is time we reclaim our feminine spirit and dare to let that spirit dance us.

May you enjoy your journey as a woman. May you dance on it all!

Acknowledgements

It was clear, almost from the beginning, that though I was to claim authorship of this book, this book is not mine alone. A Higher Power playfully arranged "meaningful coincidences" throughout the writing of the manuscript. The right people, situations, and events would appear at the precise moments they were needed. A story would unfold, sometimes humorous, sometimes poignant, each with its own unique wisdom to impart. Another chapter would be written. And so the process continued, much throughout the book. Such amazing synchronicity can come only from the hand of the Divine Mother.

In particular, I wish to acknowledge Karen Vermillion, a gifted Houston artist, who captures so poetically the expressiveness of the exquisite dance that is a woman's journey. She so sensitively portrays the fluid movement of the emerging woman who extends herself to dance with and through it all!

From Europe, there was the special blessing of Elinore Detiger, rightfully known as the "Global Mother" who, using her innate cosmic time clock, would appear in fairy-godmother fashion at just the right moment with just the right magic potion. In Holland, it was Manec van der Lugt and the nurturing energy of the women of Davidhuis who gave much-needed female support. Within the beautiful walls of my Dutch home away from home, I was lovingly coaxed and encouraged, so that the birthing process of this book could take place.

Two men deserve special thanks for their contributions, symbolic of the importance of male-female polarity and proof that men can be incredibly sensitive to the special issues of women. A heartfelt thanks first to Robert Krajenke, who endured my erratic changes and helped smooth out many a wrinkle in the manuscript with his assistance in writing and editing. A special acknowledgement also to Bud Ramey, who has deepened my understanding of friendship and who was always there to help hold the vision of the book. Without his sustaining force, this would, no doubt, still be an unwritten manuscript.

In addition, I want to acknowledge Drs. Carl and Stephanie Simonton, from whom I learned much about the transformational process possible within each of us. A special thank you goes to Carol Bush, co-creator of the original version of the Emerging Woman Seminar. And appreciation goes to Grace Davide for careful editing, to Cheri Sommers for un-told hours of typing, and to Jean Reeder and Martha Hamilton for being reliable sounding boards.

Most of all, I value my family. I was privileged to have a childhood in the foothills of the Blue Ridge Mountains, where simplicity is synonymous with beauty. My father, Guy Marlow, taught me to find the extraordinary in the ordinary; and my mother, Esther Marlow, always knew it was a joy to be a woman and passed on that wisdom. To my sons, David and John, you are both treasures; your love and encouragement ever sustain me.

The Bitch is the negative aspect of the feminine.
It is the role we
resort to when we don't know what else
to do. We use her when we don't know how to
express what we are feeling in a
confident, whole way.

The Bitch is that part of us
that is connected to our feelings of
powerlessness. We nag, grouch, whine,
withdraw, shout, or shut down because
we don't feel we have other options.

We use the Bitch to manipulate and
maneuver—and she usually gets results.
But there are better ways to get the love
and attention we deserve.

In this chapter, you will learn to clearly
identify and name your Bitch. This will enable
you to now move decisively to your real
power and true identity.

Chapter 1
Owning the Bitch

All women are magicians. Our magic is the innate ability we have to both create and transform our experiences of life. As women, our only real choices are whether or not we practice our magic consciously and how much magic we are willing to use.

It has taken me many years to understand this magic—the magic of a woman emerging from limitation into wholeness and enjoying the freedom inherent in the process. The insights come from my own journey as a woman, as well as the experiences of many women I have taught and counseled. It reflects the wisdom of women from diverse cultures and backgrounds—American women, European women, both rich and poor, educated and unlettered, old and young. Many female "teachers" have shared their insights with me. My teachers have been gifted and joyful women, angry women, enraged women, women with visions and dreams, those who are succeeding, those overwhelmed by loss and change, and those who are numb with boredom and apathy. They have been cancer patients struggling with death as well as women groping their way out of confusion while seeking new identities and ways of living. They have taught me about courage, courage to move through darkness and rise—to claim their true identity—renewed, empowered, and joyful.

Begin The Dance

The emerging process is a wonderful dance. It is a movement to wholeness and joy. There is a theme that continues to play throughout the dance, and, when you can hear that melody, it makes the movement easier, more graceful. The first step is to be willing to name the name: identify clearly where you are and what your issues are. Secondly, accept that where you are and what you have done up to this point is okay. Thirdly, be open to all the possibilities, potential, and power that are yours. The dance has many moods because you are intricate, complex, and delicate. And it will take you home to your heart, where you can finally claim full ownership of your inner authority. Move at your own pace, at your own rhythm. You may want to leave some steps until later. They are ready for you when you are ready for them.

We begin with what may seem to be one of the most challenging steps, both in the book and in our life: Owning the Bitch. This chapter is placed at the beginning for that reason. If from the beginning we can establish honesty as a requirement, then the rest will come.

For now, drop preconceived ideas about the word *Bitch*. And be open to another view. We all know that we have parts inside that we wish weren't there or that we are afraid are there. We fear they will come out when we least want them to. It is these parts that I am boldly calling the Bitch. I choose this term because it is unattractive. If it is unattractive enough, we will have to notice it. We won't be able to avoid or deny or glamorize or whitewash her behavior. But the Bitch is not our real self. She is but a caricature of our shadow self. Be mature enough to see the humor in what you do. We can really look ridiculous when we get into these patterns. What we won't resort to! Humor is healthy. We can be both responsible and lighthearted at the same time.

The Birth of a Bitch

The winter had been especially cold with heavy snow. My brother John and my sister Joanna and I were constantly sneezing, dripping, and coughing and passing our colds back and forth to one another. So it was great news when Mom and Dad announced that the family was going for a vacation, to enjoy some warm Florida sun. At last, some real excitement.

On the way south, John and I were in the back seat, acting out that ancient sibling rivalry of claiming territorial rights. In fairness to John, I believe I started the fight with a few innocent jabs. John retaliated with some serious pokes. Our wrestling and pushing continued over the next few miles until we reached the restaurant, and then it spilled over into the menu-selection ritual.

John squeezed my hand under the table and bent my fingers back. My eyes began to water and I squirmed in my seat. I was double-jointed and a lot of John's hand crunching I could tolerate without a squeal or whimper. But then he pulled too hard, and the pain became more than I could tolerate. I screamed and pulled my hand away.

Mother lowered her menu and gave us one of her stone-cold glares.

"Betty, leave John alone," she said, fixing her eyes on me.

I was outraged! Who was being hurt—John or me? I was! Without a word, I pushed my chair back and stormed away from the table. I knew that if I exploded, I would be punished. I wanted to cry, but I couldn't. I wanted to scream, but I dared not.

"Oh, Betty's on her high horse again!" I heard Mom say behind me as I walked away, and Dad smiled knowingly. Typical of many parents, they judged my behavior but didn't know how to help me deal with it.

So many feelings were churning inside me. Frustration. Anger. Hurt. And no place to put them! Something inside me was pleading to be understood, to be reassured that I was still loved. I walked to the other end of the restaurant, trying to quiet these turbulent emotions. When I had stuffed them down sufficiently to where I felt under control, I returned to the table and assumed my usual, passive, girlish attitude. The family approved, and I felt accepted. But inside, there was a live volcano ready to erupt.

A man at the next table stood up to pay his bill, and as he passed our table, he stopped to pay his compliments. "You have such an attractive family," he remarked to my mother and father. And then winking at me, he added, "That little one is something else. She's quite an actress."

A bitch was born. I was three years old at the time.

* * * *

The Bitch is our false self, and a false self can give only false power. The Bitch is something we create to cover up our fears because we lack confidence in our true selves. Settling for the

Bitch is a poor alternative to making decisions for ourselves and expressing our real feelings and needs.

* * * *

The Bitch Grows Up

At age three, it never occurred to me that I was cheating myself by creating a Bitch. In fact, it took many years to realize that the false part, the role I had assumed as a three-year-old, sitting at that table smiling while my insides were burning, was separate from my authentic self.

Thirty-five years later I looked at my Bitch square in the face and realized what I had created.

It was a hot June day, and I was upstairs in the bedroom of our spacious home on the James River, sorting out socks. The weather was humid and sticky. The cooling system had broken, so the windows were open to capture whatever little breeze might stir and relieve some of the oppressive heat.

Sock-sorting is a mindless task, something to do while thoughts dance among pleasant dreams. My peaceful interlude was abruptly interrupted when Sean, my husband, suddenly bounded through the doorway with a sense of great urgency. Often this energy, so typical of Sean, was a delightful change; other times it was an intrusion. Today it felt like the latter.

Sean started commenting on the condition of the garden. Usually, this would spark my interest. But today, as he droned on about the zinnias and the broccoli, I just kept sorting and folding, sorting and folding, pretending to be involved and interested in his monologue.

And then I heard Sean say, "Well, what do you think?"

What did I think? About what? I had no idea what he had been talking about!

I started to stammer some vague response, and then my stomach knotted. It was as though a complete stranger had just walked into my bedroom—a man off the street—and said, "You've been married to me for fifteen years."

My hands turned cold and wet, sticking to the socks I kept carefully sorting. "And I am a stranger to him." A sick shiver went through my body.

Over the years, I had tried so hard to please him. To adjust.

To adapt. To fit in. We never fought, we never argued. But what had become of the imaginative, adventurous me who was full of fire and spontaneous emotion, or the young child who had felt such curiosity and wonder? We had what everyone considered an enviable situation. Sean was the successful attorney/husband. We had two fine sons, lived in the most exclusive part of town, and were members in good standing in the Episcopal Church, the Junior League, and the country club. But why did I feel empty and unfulfilled?

For the first time, I realized the knotted stomach and clammy hands, the tense body, shallow smile, and tilted chin was the Bitch I had created. She was a whole set of reactions that came when I didn't know what to do or what to say. I had been living with this unknown Bitch ever since I sat down at the table on our way to Florida—and I was still stuck there, swallowing my feelings and doing everything that was pleasing and pleasant to get what I thought I wanted. No wonder Sean was a stranger. I was a stranger to myself!

I recognized the Bitch inside. At the same time, I knew it my was not my real Self, only the Self I had settled for. If I were to understand her, I needed to name her with words that would accurately describe her unique qualities. Instantly, the words The Pleasing Passive came to mind. That's what I had become. In due time the socks got sorted, but I had a more serious sorting out to do.

What Happens If We Don't Acknowledge The Bitch?

It is hard to admit that we possess a Bitch (or Bitches). In fact, we will usually deny, rationalize, or suppress our behavior just to prove she doesn't exist.

Failure to acknowledge our Bitch means we will continue to feel powerless, suppressed, unfulfilled, and afraid. The Bitch is the defense against our insecurities. We call on her to help us manipulate and maneuver, to get what we think we want from others. If we need attention, recognition, and reassurance in order to cover over our fears, she gets it for us. She is effective and she is powerful. But she is false power, and using her keeps us stuck in false self.

The Bitch Must Be Confronted

As children we learn that if being cute and smiling doesn't work, sulking, pouting, or silence may eventually get Mom and Dad to notice us. Or we might kick and scream and rant and rave, until we wear our parents down and they give us the attention we want out of frustration. Or we might simply decide to be "nice"—at all costs. If these childhood coping mechanisms are not dealt with, in time they become Bitches and our only adult means of coping.

Unwilling to confront our own Bitch, we may recognize her in others. Parents, partners, bosses, or friends present us with all the negative patterns that we deny within ourselves. They act out our disowned parts. In other words, if we don't deal with the inner Bitch, we'll draw one to us. What we dislike in others is within ourselves.

When a family group fails to acknowledge the shadow self, one family member invariably will act out the "craziness" the others pretend they don't have. This is the proverbial "Black sheep" of the family.

When a community fails to come to grips with its negative unconscious patterns, they are projected onto a scapegoat. The Salem Witch trials is a classic case in point. In modern times, often the Jews, Blacks, or third-world citizens are the targets for projections and become the twentieth-century scapegoats.

How To Meet The Bitch

One of the classic challenges in the ancient myths and fairy tales is meeting the hideous damsel, the stepmother, an evil fairy, or a witch. She is the one with the power to turn the heroes/heroines into stone, or put them to sleep, or cause them to lose their heads. Nothing significant happens in these tales without that kind of confrontation. The Witch—or Bitch—is the catalyst for change.

There are some subtleties in meeting the Witch. Though she often appears as an obvious hag, dark and sinister with a bent and disfigured body, crackling voice, and beady eyes, other times she disguises herself in forms that appear harmless, alluring, or seductive. Snow White, for example, was tricked into eating the poisonous apple because her evil mother-in-law disguised herself as a harmless old woman.

In many fairy tales, the Witch is encountered in the depths of a dark green forest, a murky and sinister place. It takes courage to enter it and often the pathway back or out is lost. Hansel and Gretel carefully leave a trail of bread crumbs behind them, and birds eat them up. It is as though once the decision has been made to meet her, there is no turning back!

As women, we too must be willing to go into our own dark green forest of the unconscious to meet the shadow self, the negative feminine. The confrontation and acknowledgement of that part of the psyche is an important step in the process of becoming whole.

Every woman, on her path to wholeness, has the same challenges of initiation, integration, and transformation as the characters in the old folktales. The murky, ominous forest where the Bitch is met is the darkness of our own unconscious which we fear to enter. But until we do, the Witch's power is unchallenged.

The Power of the Name

To defuse the power of the Bitch, we must identify or name her.

The belief in the power of names is evident in many major religions and in the ancient stories. Words of power attend great events. As with Ali Baba's words, the name opens doors magically.

One of the best illustrations of the ancient principle of "naming the name" is from Grimm's fairy tale, *Rumpelstiltskin.*

A poor miller foolishly boasts to the king that his daughter can spin straw into gold. The king, ever eager for more wealth, immediately puts her to the test. He locks her in a room filled with straw and a spinning wheel and demands that she turn the straw into gold.

The terrified girl sits at her spinning wheel, sobbing and wailing with no idea how to proceed, when a curious little dwarf appears and offers his magic. However, she must agree to make payment for his help.

The dwarf asks for her necklace in exchange for his help. She gladly acquiesces. As promised, he magically spins the straw into gold.

The next morning, when the greedy king discovers the room is filled with gold, he orders more straw brought in and demands she turn it into gold also.

The dwarf appears again and asks for her ring. She agrees, and again the dwarf turns the straw to purest gold. When the king returns, he is ecstatic! He has the room filled with even more straw and demands her to again, overnight, spin the straw into gold.

This time, when the dwarf appears, he demands her first-born child as his due. She agrees because she has nothing left to give.

In the morning, the king is so pleased with all the gold that he marries the miller's daughter. Within a year they have a child.

One day, as she is rocking her newborn son, the dwarf comes to collect his payment. She pleads with him to allow her to keep her child. Moved to pity by her tears, he offers a way out. If she can discover his name within three days, she can keep her child.

For three days, she plays a desperate guessing game with the dwarf, trying to discover his name, but without success. On the third day, the queen's faithful servant discovers the dwarf's home high in the mountains at the end of the forest and spies, unnoticed, while the dwarf dances gleefully around the fire, chanting "Rumpelstiltskin is my name."

In the evening, the dwarf comes to the palace to claim the child. Once again, he asks the queen to tell him his name. When she pronounces the word of power, "Rumpelstiltskin," the dwarf destroys himself in a rage.

In fairy tales as in dreams, a dwarf can represent stunted growth, an aspect of unfulfilled potential which exists within the unconscious. As long as his name was a secret—his true essence or identity concealed—Rumpelstiltskin was in control.

Once the miller's daughter "named the name," she got to keep her child, the symbol of her personal power. The principle illustrated here is that when we can name or identify something, we gain power over it. To know the name of a person, object, or situation is to correctly identify its essence. And by knowing its essence you can establish an effective relationship with it. When I recognized my Bitch as a "Pleasing Passive," I identified a false part of myself that I was using to gain acceptance and appreciation. By knowing her name, I could dismiss her power and diminish her influence. It was an important step toward owning real power.

Name Your Bitch

In this section, you will have an opportunity to regain your power by naming the Bitch.

Most women, from time to time, have expressed the behavior of one or more of the Bitches described below. No doubt, one or two will strike a particularly familiar note in you. As you read, recognize which ones most describe your behavior and then try "Naming the Bitch" at the end of the chapter.

Bitches come in many guises. There are Bitches to suit every temperament, personality, and preference. Bitches abound!

Here are twenty variations:

ICY MAIDEN

"I said there's nothing wrong. . . (But you better know how I feel anyway.)"

She is the woman who is cold, unattainable, sometimes haughty. She keeps her power by withholding her energy. Her heart is hidden and closed off. Her fear—although it may be subconscious—is that if she ever really opens herself up and becomes vulnerable, she will be used or abandoned. The Icy Maiden creates a sense of safety for herself by shutting off her feelings. This Bitch avoids strong emotions. Anger, resentments, embarrassment, helplessness, etc., only produce conflicts and discomfort.

She chooses not to feel anything at all. By avoiding her feelings, she gets to keep her control. Icy stares, folded arms, the "pull-away," and pursed lips are all a part of her game.

"Nothing is wrong" is her cold shutdown. The game she plays is called "You're supposed to love me enough to know what's wrong without my telling you—and if you don't, I'm going to shut down even more." The game is subtle, deliberate, and carefully executed.

"I won't give myself to you because I'm not getting what I want from you." Her power is in withholding and making others strive to get her love.

CASTRATING FEMALE

"Wait till I get through with this son of a bitch!"

The Castrating Female is powerful and ruthless, sarcastic, disempowering, and belittling. She takes great delight in emasculating men with her sharp tongue, testy jabs, and barbs.

"Oh, George, now really!" or "You're going to do what? You've got to be kidding!"

She is equally skillful in her use of disarming body language and stony stares.

She shows great disgust toward her mate. After all, "He's not a real man, just a wimp!" As long as she keeps him lifeless, she can feel powerful.

SHRIEKING WAR GODDESS

"Just what the hell do you mean by that!"

The Shrieking War Goddess is highly manipulative and overpowering. Filled with explosive anger and enormous rage, she rants and raves to get control and attacks at the slightest provocation.

No matter who is plundered and raped in the process, she challenges, "Let's get it all out," often amidst yells and screams. As one woman in a workshop boasted, "I don't have a bit of trouble with anger. I just let it out." And she did, at great cost to all around her.

Women who suppress their anger often harbor a Shrieking War Goddess. They have not learned to deal with issues as they come up. Instead, they avoid trouble until their suppressed rage becomes too powerful. Then the dam bursts, and the flood is enormous.

MERCILESS MERMAID

"Come and get me. . .if you can."

Mermaids are mysterious mythological creatures, half fish, half woman. Mermaids are the epitome of heartless, impersonal eroticism. Her aim is to conquer men, not for love but for a craving to gain power. Her rage and desire to disempower is disguised by an exceedingly personable manner and apparent concern. The Mermaid is the proverbial "cock-tease" who only craves the game.

The power in wanting to be wanted is secondary to her greatest power, which lies in turning the man down at the critical moment, or just shutting her own energy off, and watching his confusion. Often, this pattern is a result of abusive exploitation early in life and it is an attempt to get back at men in general.

SACCHARINE BELLE

"Why honey, everything is just fine."

We associate this Bitch with the deep South, but, in truth, she is found everywhere. Everything is sweet and sugary to the point of being repugnant. Real feelings and opinions are covered by a sugar-coated exterior shell. But it is not real sugar, just a "substitute." It is all a role, a superficial game. The smile is plastic, the conversation predictable.

"Well, how are you? I am so glad to see you."

"And how is your mother? Really, I am so glad!"

"Now you really must come and see us. We would love to see you!"

The little magnolia blossom has charmed everyone, though there is little real caring in the script. The words are effective. It does work, and it gets results, including important invitations and the prestige of being "in" with the right people. Scarlett O'Hara in *Gone With The Wind* knew quite well how to become the Saccharine Belle when she needed something for her beloved plantation, Tara.

SUFFERING MARTYR

"That's all right. . .(sigh). . .I'll do it."

She is the woman who prides herself on stoic self-denial, martyring herself for her husband, her children, "the Cause," or her career. She holds back her anger and her sexuality and suppresses her joy. She wins her points by suffering the most and letting everybody be aware of how much she hurts.

She believes suffering makes her special. She chooses the opportune moments to sigh loudly, so as to maximize the effect. She vacuums noisily or straightens up the room when the rest of the family is watching the Superbowl! That way, everyone will be sure to notice "good ole mom" working away again.

One woman who recalls playing the role of the Suffering Martyr remembers a Thanksgiving dinner with enough seats for everyone except herself. When asked where she was going to sit, she replied, "Oh, no, I won't sit down. I just want to be sure that everyone else is taken care of!"

Everyone feels obligated to a Suffering Martyr. She dominates through her pain. From this highly manipulative and controlling position, she wields a lot of power. Veiled behind the suffering is usually a belief that she doesn't deserve love and nurturing.

She has yet to learn that she doesn't need to suffer to get love.

This behavior presents a seeming paradox that must be understood. True giving is a virtue that must come from a generous heart. If we give to impress others or to appear virtuous, we are operating with an ulterior motive. If we give because we feel we're supposed to, it's hell. Then we are indeed the Suffering Martyr.

PLEASING PASSIVE

"Whatever you say, dear."

Quiet, demure, agreeable, and compliant, this Bitch copes by becoming invisible, by not being noticed, or by not making waves or demands. The Pleasing Passive has given up original thought and personal opinions in the hope that she will not be objectionable and lose the approval of others.

One of the most startling examples of the Pleasing Passive was in a workshop that I was conducting in Holland. We were doing an exercise in which one partner allows another to push them until they turn around, face their partner directly, and say, "Stop, that's enough!" Body language and the manner in which the words are delivered reveal much about how a woman deals with her anger. In this particular instance, one woman allowed herself to be pushed clear across the room. She then turned and politely said, "Thank you." Our ingrained patterns run deep!

Usually, enormous rage is locked up behind the Pleasing Passive pattern. A very sweet but painfully sad young woman once came for counseling. She was hunched over and suffering from migraine headaches. When she was growing up, her father had abused her both physically and emotionally. She was angry and terrified of expressing any anger, since her only model for expressing deep-felt emotions had been such a negative one.

To defuse the volcano that wanted to erupt, she needed a safe environment within which to experience her deep pain. Once trust was established between the two of us, we put a pillow on a bed and she began to pummel that pillow with her fists. She continued beating the pillow, releasing some of her hurt and grief. Suddenly, her migraine completely cleared. Releasing her long repressed anger was an important first step. Next she must learn healthy ways to communicate her feelings.

THE SEDUCTIVE SIREN

"This one's a challenge, but I'll get him."

In the myth *Odysseus*, Circe warns Odysseus not to be lured by the song of the Sirens, the enticing sounds sung by the maidens on the islands which they would pass. Circe knew that these Sirens led to the undoing of men. Nevertheless, Odysseus's men are lured onto the island and seduced into a powerless state where sex and pleasure rule.

The Seductive Siren is out to seduce men into sexual encounters, so she uses all of her feminine charms to entice and interest them. She wants the attention of men for the assurance of her own sexuality and to gain importance in the eyes of other women. Though she does give freely of her body, she holds back her inner self. Her game is not real intimacy, but conquest. She wonders, "Am I still attractive? Can I still get him?"

Remember, Cleopatra was so enticing that wars were waged on her behalf!

MOTHER SUPERIOR

"I told you so. If only you had listened."

She is self-righteous, a know-it-all who can back up all her opinions and does not like to be questioned. The effect on those around her can be chilling. It is as though, in her presence, something inside becomes diminished and shrinks.

She maintains rigid control of herself and the situation. Her standards of right and wrong are strict. She has little tolerance for "gray" areas. Mother Superiors are female drill sergeants and overbearing mothers, school teachers, head nurses, camp counselors, and corporate executives. In whatever position they are found, above all else, a Mother Superior needs to be "right." If she discovers she has made an error, she will go to great lengths to cover herself so she won't appear wrong, which would, in her eyes, jeopardize her infallible position.

ARMORED AMAZON

"I'm as good as any man—and you better believe it!"

The Armored Amazon is that woman who identifies with the power aspect of the masculine. At the same time, she renounces the capacity to relate lovingly, a quality that has traditionally been associated with the feminine. Usually, the Amazon woman is a high achiever. She has made her way in the medical profession, the legal world, or the world of stocks and bonds. She is as good as or better than any man. Her masculine side is highly developed and provides for competence, confidence, and aggression, but the feminine qualities of nurturing and sensitivity are underdeveloped and repressed. According to Linda Leonard in *The Wounded Woman*, this Bitch is often the result of a wound in the father-daughter relationship, present in women whose fathers were "negligent or irresponsible, or not emotionally present."

The armor is her safeguard. Usually, there is a chink in the armor. If someone dare find their way into that chink, the Armored Amazon is forced to deal with emotional issues, often with great difficulty.

GOLD DIGGER

"He meets all of my qualifications—he's filthy rich!"

Though more frequently found during an earlier period of history, Gold diggers are still around. This woman is out for what she can get. If he doesn't have a Diner's Club card, membership in an elite country club, and a yacht, she is not interested. What can he buy for her? What will he give her? Real feelings of love are purely secondary. Money is where it's at. The Gold Digger, not knowing what real love is, settles for the greenbacks as her love substitute. Zsa Zsa Gabor has entertained us all with her stories of her millionaire husbands, proof that for some, "Diamonds are still a girl's best friend."

BLACK WIDOW

"I like it when they squirm."

This woman enjoys wounding the male. Her underlying question is, "Do you love me enough to let me hurt you?" She methodically coaxes, then ensnares the man in her web. Once she has completed her ritual, she is ready for the lethal sting. It is deadly.

This pattern appears most frequently when a woman has been abused and rejected by her father. The wound is deep, and she wants revenge. Since her father is not around, she gets back at him through the males she encounters. She feels quite triumphant when she ends a relationship, leaving the man to deal with the pain and rejection.

In a counseling session recently, a young woman described in a rather cool manner the great pain her former partner was having because she decided to break off the relationship. There was almost a gleeful note in her description. He was suffering, and that proved he really loved her!

In her childhood, she shared a bedroom with her sister. Her father periodically came into the bedroom and sexually abused the sister. For years she felt rage at this abuse, but it wasn't until several sessions later that we uncovered the deeper cause of the rage. Her father hadn't chosen her!

With the termination of her relationship with her partner, she learned how much suffering she could cause. Though her father didn't love her enough to make her feel powerful, her suffering partner did. She had power to attract and destroy! This way, she could vicariously punish the father who hadn't chosen her.

RESCUE ME

"Maybe he's the one."

This is the classic little girl waiting for Prince Charming to come and rescue her. Or, as an older friend of mine put it, "Where the hell is Errol Flynn?" This Bitch believes that men have all the power and she has none. If she lucks into a worthwhile relationship, life can go well for her. If, on the other hand, she surrenders herself to a not-so-wonderful male, she will endure a lot of pain—anything rather than be without a man.

Sarah, an attractive thirty-five-year-old woman, is desperate because she has been divorced ten years and still—"no one!" Recently, she met an older man at a conference who was separated from his wife. There was immediate chemistry and they shared some magical time together. Now all of her hopes are built around the possibility of this time—this is it! She has considered relocating closer to him, even though his divorce is not yet final, and he has yet to start dealing with the many inner issues that come up after separation from a long-term relationship. If this new relationship doesn't turn out with a wedding and a tiered cake, she will be devastated. The Rescue Me Bitch constantly chooses to give her right to happiness over to men, and then, when it doesn't work out, feels unfairly victimized.

ALL FEATHERS NO BIRD

"Say, What?"

This female is daffy, disorganized, flighty, irrelevant, and undirected. Often she is imaginative, adventuresome, intuitive, and mystical. She can be quite engaging with her airy lightness. Goldie Hawn was once frequently cast in this role in the movies. The underlying belief of many women who play this role is that it is not O.K. to be bright. Intelligence must be camouflaged. This affected disguise is an attempt to be nonthreatening to men, and the helplessness can be quite disarming.

This bird warbles her flighty tunes to men: "I never could read these instruction books. How do you work this thing?" or "Does the key go here?. . .I don't get it."

Many men want to be needed, and this damsel definitely appears to be in need!

WILTING BITCH

"I give up. I can't handle it!"

The Wilting Bitch seems so helpless and loves to make you feel responsible for her.

"Gee, you're wonderful. I wish I could be the good mother that you are. Kids just wear me out."

She enjoys getting depressed. This way she gets others to come and rescue her by getting her out of her mood. If nobody rallies to her aid, she will remain inactive and depressed and will bemoan the situation. Sometimes, this Bitch shows herself only in a crisis, remaining fully camouflaged at all other times.

RECONSTRUCTED BITCH

"I can really get into that."

She is the New Age groupie that has been through every process in the books. She has had her family reconstructed. She has been ESTed, Rolfed, Reikied, and Re-Birthed. She's had aromatherapy and Bach Remedies. She's been Gestalted, had psychic readings and past life regressions. Her pastime is dropping names of the teachers and groups she knows and talking "the talk." The Reconstructed Bitch has it together, or so she wants to have everyone think. She comes to take the seminars and the trainings, but not to learn from them. She knows it all, and has done it all—everything, that is, except change.

BITTER BITCH

"After all I did for you. . .and what do I get?"

The Bitter Bitch hates herself. She is unkind to herself and to others. In some families, the Bitter Bitch is an inheritance, something a bitter mother passes on to her daughters by filling their ears with how hard it is to be a woman or beliefs about how awful men and sex are. If her daughter should have any pain in her relationships with men, she will respond with the predictable "I told you so."

Often, the woman who has been left plays the role of the Bitter Bitch. A man's second wife can become a Bitter Bitch as well, especially if there are financial problems or troubles with the children of the first wife.

Deborah, an attractive thirty-year-old, closed her eyes and visualized her Bitch. She had named it and described it, and now the Bitch was right there with her. With a degree of courage, she visualized herself walking over to her bitch, a horrible, pathetic, wretched woman. Deborah looked at this disgusting form and asked, "What is it that you want me to know? What do you need?"

The answer came back clearly: "Love and attention."

Part of her feminine spirit had been denied. Her inner woman felt martyred, sacrificed, unwanted, and bitter as a result. Using her imagination, Deborah held the hands of this inner woman and poured love and caring into the pathetic form. The haggard old woman turned into a younger version of herself, vibrant, alive, energetic. The transformation was startling! When we can accept and love the negative self, it no longer has power over us.

NAGGING BITCH

"For God's sake, Henry, put the top back on the toothpaste." Nothing ever dies with the Nagging Bitch, and she never tires of trying to prove her point. She is the resurrector of the past, of old wounds, hurts, disappointments, and betrayals (real or imagined). The Nagging Bitch goes on and on about the same things. She carries a "Black Bag" full of past experiences. Critical, complaining, a whiner in relationships with men, she plays the hypercritical parent. With unnerving accuracy, she knows just how to push your buttons.

TWO-FACED BITCH

"Of course, I will. . .(You bastard, I'll get you for this!)" The Two-Faced Bitch is all smiles in your presence and all complaints behind your back. For example, she is the daughter-in-law who is cordial when his parents are visible and instantaneously switches character once they leave.

In the corporate world, the Two-Faced Bitch really wants to ruin you, but you'd never suspect it. She is too clever to reveal her true feelings. The face she puts on may be very pretty, and her words are almost always what you want to hear; but there is a seething conflict underneath. She plays a dangerous game of manipulation and deceit.

QUEEN BEE

"I'm in charge here—and don't you forget it!" The Queen Bee rules the roost and commands attention. She is the center of the universe, and everything and everyone must revolve around her. At the office she will often side with men against women and is often responsible for keeping other women from advancing. The office is her turf, and she wants everyone to know it. She uses the politics of her network to roust out undesirables who do not accept her authority as she sees it.

At home, she is the manipulating parent. When she is a grandma, she still rules during visits to the children and grandchildren. She immediately takes over the house and begins making all the decisions for the family. If she is questioned or challenged, she pouts and acts deeply hurt until she is restored to her rightful place as the Queen Bee.

Naming The Bitch

Read the list of Bitches. In the appropriate blank space, note the frequency with which these bitches appear in your life and describe the situations where you use them.

And if you are feeling really courageous, ask a friend for input!

The Bitch	Qualities	Frequency of Use					Situations When You Still Use Her
		Used To	Never	Sometimes	Often	Always	
ICY MAIDEN	"I said there is nothing wrong...(but you better know how I feel anyway)."						
CASTRATING FEMALE	"Wait until I get through with this son of a bitch."						
SHRIEKING WAR GODDESS	"Just What the hell do you mean by that?"						
SEDUCTIVE MERMAID	"Come and get me . . . if you can."						
SACCHARINE BELLE	"Why honey, everything is just fine."						

The Bitch	Qualities	Frequency of Use					Situations When You Still Use Her
		Used To	Never	Sometimes	Often	Always	
SUFFERING MARTYR	"Oh, that's all right...sigh...I'll do it anyway."						
PLEASING PASSIVE	"Whatever you say, dear."						
SEDUCTIVE SIREN	"This one's a challenge, but I will get him."						
MOTHER SUPERIOR	"I told you so. If you had only listened."						
ARMORED AMAZON	"I'm as good as any man . . .and you better believe it."						
GOLD DIGGER	"He meets all of my qualifications . . . he's filthy rich."						
BLACK WIDOW	"I like it when they squirm."						
RESCUE ME	"Maybe he's the one."						
ALL FEATHERS & NO BIRD	"Say what?"						

The Bitch	Qualities	Frequency of Use					Situations When You Still Use Her
		Used To	Never	Sometimes	Often	Always	
WILTING BITCH	"I give up . . . I just can't handle it."						
RECON-STRUCTED BITCH	"I can really get into that."						
BITTER BITCH	"After all I did for you and what did I get?"						
NAGGING BITCH	"For God's sake Henry, put the top back on the toothpaste."						
TWO-FACED BITCH	"Of course I will...(You bastard, I'll get you for this.)"						
QUEEN BEE	"I'm in charge here and don't you forget it."						

The Dragon Fight is the age-old conflict in
establishing our own identities. The dragon
is the symbol for the parents. The Dragon Fight
begins early in life and can be life-long.
At the heart of the fight is the issue of our own
individualities, our struggles to be authentic.

The Dragon Fight is the struggle we have with
ourselves when we rebel against our parents or strive
to emulate them. Either way, there is a fight.
The Dragon fight ends when we
are willing to accept our parents the way
they are, allow ourselves to be who we are,
and complete the job of parenting for ourselves.

Healing the Dragon Fight helps you understand
your parents. It also gets you in touch
with your issues surrounding
masculine and feminine energy and your
relationship patterns.

Chapter 2
Ending the
Dragon Fight

I remember as a child lying on a grassy bank on a hot summer evening, smelling the honeysuckle, gazing at the star-filled sky and wondering: Who am I? Where did I come from? Why was I born? Of all the possible places I could be, why am I living in this small town? And, why, of all the people on earth, am I with these parents?

As I sat on that grassy bank, I thought, "I must be adopted." The notion was strangely comforting for me, an explanation my young mind could easily grasp. After all, my brothers and sister were dark while I was blonde and fair. And certainly I carried a different inner spirit.

"Mother, are you sure I am not adopted?" It was a question I asked more than once.

"Betty, really! Why do you keep asking that!" she'd reply with an air of peevishness. "Why would I adopt you, when I already had two children?"

Nevertheless, I wasn't convinced. I didn't feel I belonged. We weren't like a mother and daughter should be. And certainly there were times I thought that if I could have chosen my parents, I would have picked differently. Not that there wasn't love. There was. But my father, as loving as he was, was much too old-fashioned and restrictive for my spontaneous, adventurous nature. And mother. Well, that's where the battle really was. Sometimes a mother has one particular child that is her main challenge. I was definitely the one.

I wanted to take dance; mother insisted on piano. When I wanted to wear make-up. she thought I was too young. We battled over privacy, curfews, hairstyle, choice of friends, everything! Or so it seemed. When I fell in love for the very first time, she refused to let Jimmy and me see each other. She didn't approve. In her eyes, he didn't measure up.

I was equally critical of her. Must she always wear heels, even when washing the clothes! Couldn't she, just once, be like other mothers and go to the grocery store in slacks? Did we always have to have "healthy" food? Did the rules have to be so rigid? Couldn't she appreciate my friends as much as I did?

On that grassy bank, I felt very alone and certain that I was the only girl who had these problems, the only one who struggled so intensely with her parents, the only one with a dragon to fight.

Life as a Mystery School

Our parents were not perfect people, but they were the perfect parents for us. Consider the possibility that, before you were born, a Divine Intelligence allowed you to choose your parents, and you specifically chose the ones you have. Assume that you chose your parents because you recognized something about them that made them the perfect parents, the perfect teachers for whatever lessons, strengths, virtues, talents, or abilities you needed to develop in order to become whole in this life. Living as though that were true might change your perspective about your relationship with your parents.

Every person, every situation we encounter in life presents us with an opportunity to learn something about ourselves. Life is a school, and we, by virtue of being on the planet, are automatically enrolled as students. In this School of Life our "teachers" are all the people in our lives who reflect or mirror back aspects of ourselves.

As teachers, their job is to help us to become more conscious. The requirement for graduation is "Know thyself." Sometimes, the stronger our reaction to a person, the more valuable the teacher.

Consider the possibility that your parents are important faculty members in this school. They have set up a curriculum and initiated lessons for your development and spiritual growth that you will be attempting to master for many years, if not for your entire life.

Parents act, mirror, exaggerate, and reflect whatever it is we need to learn. When we no longer react to those aspects of our parents that once triggered us and can respond instead, we have mastered our lesson. It no longer holds power over us.

The Dragon Fight

In myths and fairy tales, one of the archetypal tasks of the hero or heroine is to slay a dragon. The dragon is usually a ferocious, fire-breathing monster, big and powerful, often guarding a treasure. He makes people cower in fear and keeps them from experiencing and expressing life fully.

Art therapist Joan Kellogg, in her book *Mandala: Path of Beauty*, uses the term "Dragon Fight" to describe the age-old conflict that children have in establishing their own identities. The dragon is the symbol for the parents. The Dragon Fight begins early in life and can be life-long. At the heart of the Fight is the issue of our own individualities, our struggles to become our authentic selves.

* * * *

The Dragon Fight is the struggle we have with ourselves when we rebel against our parents or strive to emulate them. Either way, there is a fight.

The Dragon Fight ends when we are willing to let our parents be who they are and when we can let ourselves be who we are and complete the job of parenting for ourselves.

* * * *

Throughout our most formative and dependent years, our mother and father, or whoever plays the role of primary caretaker, are the only models we have of the world. They give us our first concepts of who we are. They are also our primary role models for what it means to be male and female and what it means to be in relationship.

The moment we start to feel that our parents aren't giving us all that we need, the battle begins. If we feel disappointed or cheated in life because of the parents we have, we may wonder, "Why was I born to them!" We become critical and resentful or ashamed and embarrassed. We reject them and rebel by becoming the opposite of everything they stand for. Or, we will strive to emulate them, making ourselves over in their images in order to gain acceptance and approval.

Either way, we are fighting dragons. We have not differentiated ourselves from them and accepted ourselves. We feel unloved and insecure. The relationship with our parents stops developing. We may remain the fearful child, the rebellious daughter, or the blaming adolescent for life.

Though the Dragon Fight is about parents, we don't always fight it out with our parents. Whatever has been unresolved with our parents carries over into other relationships. Someone else may be playing the mother role or may be the father figure for us: husband, lover, children, bosses, teachers, the bus driver, or the sales clerk. Whatever we wanted and didn't get from our parents, we will try to get from them.

You are still in a relationship with your parents even if they are thousands of miles away, even if you haven't made contact with them since childhood, and even if they are deceased. You still carry your relationship inside you. That relationship colors your outlook in every area of your life. It affects the way you look at yourself, the way you feel about your own femininity and masculinity, and the way you respond in all your relationships.

One of the saddest things is watching seventy- and eighty-year-old cancer patients crying on their deathbeds over unresolved relationships with their parents. The need to come to resolution is so deep that after a lifetime of the Dragon Fight, there is a last attempt to end it. Outward battle or inner struggle, the fight goes on until the dragon is slain.

The Parent Picture

Draw your mother and father on a sheet of paper using colored pencils or crayons. Draw them as people, not symbols. (In other words, don't make your parent a star or a tree or a rainbow.)

It doesn't matter if you know how to draw or not. Even stick figures can reveal helpful information. The key is to be spontaneous.

Through spontaneous or impromptu drawings, the unconscious expresses itself and often communicates more clearly than through our rational processes.

Complete your drawing before turning to the next section. Reading ahead may alter your experience.

What The Parent Picture Means

It's Really You

While your Parent Picture is about your parents, everything that you draw is really about yourself. (This will be discussed in greater detail later in this chapter.) The Parent Picture gives information in four specific areas:

1. How you see your parents

In order to identify and resolve old patterns, you need to be honest about your feelings toward your parents. The drawings will reflect not necessarily who your parents are but who you think they are. What do the drawings say about the interaction they had with each other? To themselves? To you?

2. Your relationship patterns

We learn about relationships from our parents. In the drawings, how close or separate are your parents? What are their hidden agendas? What kind of scripting did you get about relationships? In what way are you repeating their same patterns?

(Look for same or opposite patterns.) For example, if your father is a "rageaholic," you may attract the same pattern or an opposite pattern, someone totally shut off from feelings. Either way, you are still dealing with the same issue. The more dysfunctional the pattern, the more desperate the attempt to recreate the same pattern. It is our misplaced effort to heal the original pattern.

3. Your female-male balance

The figures in your Parent Picture represent your feminine and masculine qualities and how integrated and balanced they are.

FEMININE	MASCULINE
Gentle	Strong
Right-Brain	Left-Brain
Feelings	Logic
Emotions	Reasoning

Receptive	Assertive
Spontaneous	Organized
Nurturing	Protective
Scattered	Disciplined
Wisdom	Knowledge
Vulnerable	Rigid
Understanding	Judgment
Moon	Sun
Unconscious	Conscious
Cold	Hot
Introverted	Extroverted
Intuitive	Pragmatic
Form	Force
Spatial	Linear

Look at your parents drawing and determine the feminine and masculine qualities of each parent. Which of these qualities have you owned? Which qualities are missing?

4. What you need to do in complete the job of parenting yourself. For example:
Is the mother too rigid?
    You need more flexibility.
A parent has no feet.
    You need more roots, grounding.
Is the father too serious?
    Your male side and/or the men in your life
    either tend to be too serious or not
    serious enough.

It takes both training and intuition to interpret all the subtleties of the drawings. For example, which colors and/or combination of colors can add another dimension to the level of interpretation? But even without training, the following guidelines can give you enough information to learn a great deal from your Parent Picture.

Interpreting Your Drawing: Things to Look For

Mood

What is the overall mood of your parents? Are they somber, rigid, open? Is that how you express yourself?

Roles

A. Take your drawing and crease it down the middle. Usually the mother is on the left and the father is on the right. If they are reversed, what does this tell you about who played which role in your life? Did "male" and "female" get switched for you? Do you attract "masculine" women or "feminine" men?

B. Which of your parents dominates? If one of the parents is noticeably weak, who in your life plays that role for you now? (For example, women who draw a small or insignificant father figure will usually attract either very weak men or overbearing "macho" types in their lives.) Or if one parent is weak, do you play the weak role in relationships?

C. How close or separated are your parents from each other? Are they connected or are they distant? If they are connected, do they seem enmeshed or comfortably supportive?

What does the picture say about how you relate to significant men/women in your life now?

How integrated are your male and female aspects?

Body Language

A. How much of your parents did you draw? (Just the head, the head and shoulders, etc.) How well do you know your parents? How well do you know yourself?

B. What part of their bodies has the most focus? Look for any part of the body that stands out. What parts of the body are emphasized and which parts are weak or undeveloped? How accurate are your drawings? (If your father was slim, did you draw him fat? If your mother was flat-chested, did you draw her with a bosom?)

Look for symbolic interpretations of the body. If you drew your father with no ears, for example, that may mean that you felt he never "heard" you. If your mother has an ample bosom, you may have felt her to be very nurturing.

Symbols And Their Common Associations

Clenched Jaw

Unexpressed feelings, overly self-controlled.

Ears

Unless covered with long hair, they should be present. If they are missing, it could indicate whether you felt listened to or not.

Hair

Hair represents thoughts. Is the hair wild, controlled, free, tight?

Eyes

Eyes represent how you see things. What are the feelings, the expression conveyed through the eyes (fear, anger, suspicion, etc.)?

Round eyes suggest love or warmth. Deep-set eyes suggest a critical thinker.

Mouth

The mouth symbolizes communication. Full lips usually indicate someone who likes to share verbally.

Thin, tight lips suggest emotions or thoughts that are withheld.

Neck

This is the connector between the mind and emotions, or the head and the heart. If the neck is extremely long, it may indicate pride. No neck can be indicative of someone who has trouble connecting his head with his heart. If there are restrictions around the neck (scarves, collars, necklaces, etc.), there is usually difficulty in verbal expression.

Shoulders

Burdens are carried on the shoulders. If shoulders are too broad, the person may carry too many burdens. Hunched-up shoulders can indicate fear. Shoulders that are in proper proportion to the body frame may indicate someone who is responsible and trustworthy.

Arms

Ability to express, to reach out. Are the arms rigid, hands in pockets, locked behind the body? This could indicate the parent was not able to give or receive. Do you have those issues?

Elbows

A graceful bend to the elbows suggests flexibility, adaptability; stiffness suggests a rigidity of self-expression.

Torso

This part of the body reflects the sense of self. A slumping position indicates lack of self-worth. A protruding or overly large torso, in proportion to the rest of the body, indicates an overbearing nature, or someone who is "puffed up" with self.

Bosom

This indicates the ability to be warm and nurturing. Notice whether you drew your mother with large breasts, though in real life she may have very small breasts. A very flat chest usually indicates unwillingness to be a woman and a desire instead to remain a little girl.

Solar Plexus

The solar plexus is the area of the adrenals, the seat of our emotions. If there is a lot of emphasis in this area in the drawing, it can indicate emotional issues that need to be worked through or emotions that need to be expressed. Look particularly for tight or oversized belts. This can suggest repressed sexuality, a condition of keeping everything tight and under control.

Legs

Legs are what we stand on and represent foundation and support. Look to see whether legs are out of proportion to the rest of the body (too large or too small).

Weak, underdeveloped legs indicate a weak foundation.

Sluggish legs denote difficulty in initiating action.

Thick or overly muscular legs reflect brute force.

Feet

Feet give us balance. They represent physical or psychological grounding. Look to see if the feet are on the ground. A drawing on tiptoes or with feet off-balance indicates that the person has a hard time making contact physically or psychologically with life. These people tend to be dreamers. Feet that do not touch the ground indicate someone who is "up in the air."

What direction are the feet pointing (away from or toward the male or female figures)? Feet are also how and where we move in our lives.

Parent Picture Reflections

1. What does your drawing tell you about how you see your parents?

2. How does this picture reflect your most significant female/male relationship patterns (past or present)? Is your current or recent relationship similar to your parents? The same? Opposite? Does it represent an earlier pattern, but one you have moved beyond?

3. The next level is to internalize your drawing. Remember that the mother and father you drew also relates to your feminine/masculine aspects.

Now look at your drawing as a picture of yourself. What does it suggest about your male and female sides? Which side looks stronger, happier, underdeveloped, weak, dominant, etc.?

4. What does your picture suggest about what you need to do for yourself in order to become more balanced and whole?

Parenting Yourself

Write in the spaces below. Use extra paper if necessary.

1. What didn't your parents do for you?

2. Why didn't they do it?

3. What do you wish they had done?

4. What difference would that have made?

After answering these questions, remind yourself that *your parents have done their job*. Whatever was not done by them is now up to you to complete for yourself.

5. How can you complete the job of parenting yourself now?

Creating Our Parents

We create our parents! None of us have the same parents we were born to. Of course, we have the same biological parents. That can't be changed. But the mother, the father you have today are the ones that you created as a result of your experience with them.

To illustrate, take a moment and imagine that you and your parents are sitting down together at a large table. You have a sheet of paper in front of you that says "Describe the three most outstanding traits of your parents."

In front of your parents are sheets also. They are to describe what they consider their three most outstanding traits.

What are the three things that you put on your list? Are they the same ones you would have had when you were five years old? When you were a teenager? Five years ago? Six months ago? Will those same traits be the ones you will see in them five years from now?

What did your parents write on their list? How did they describe themselves? Is their list the same as yours? Or do they see themselves differently than you see them?

Who are your parents? The ones you made up? Or are they who they think they are? Or could it be that who they really are goes beyond the awareness of both you and your parents?

One thing is clear. We all have beliefs and opinions about our mothers and fathers, and these come out of our experiences with them. Our relationships with our parents are colored by these beliefs and opinions. And beliefs can be changed. Therefore our experiences—past, present, and future—can all be changed. That is part of the magic we have—the power to transform.

No Two Parents Are The Same!

Several years ago, two sisters took the *Emerging Woman Seminar* in Washington, D.C. When it came time for the Parent Picture, the results were astounding!

Marlene, the older sister, using dark colors, drew her father as austere and remote. Everything about her drawing suggested her father was closed and aloof. His hands were in his pockets, his head was turned away, and there was a significant space separating the two figures. On the other hand, Meryl, the younger sister, drew a light, bright, cheerful man with a smile on his face with his arms open invitingly at his side. Could this be the same person?

The portraits of their mother also reflected contrasting points of view. Marlene drew her mother with light, bright colors. She was attractive and well-proportioned and projected a warm and sunny disposition—a born nurturer. Meryl pictured her mother as a puffy, bloated, tight-lipped woman, glowering through tense, slit eyes with her hands on her hips in rigid and judgmental posture. A frightening harridan!

Children from the same family will have different experiences and relationships with the same set of parents, as their parents will with them. But with Marlene and Meryl, the differences were extreme. The two pictures were so totally dissimilar that it would be impossible to guess that they represented the same set of parents.

For Marlene, the mother was the available one, warm and touchable. For Meryl, the father had been the primary nurturer. Same parents—different realities.

Hidden Dragons: The Saint-Sinner Syndrome

Some of the dragons we face are obvious ones. We are aware of which issues are raised as we interact with a particular parent. We have insights into how they mirror us. Being conscious of our own process and taking responsibility for our part in it indicates we are well on our way to ending the fight.

The real challenge comes, though, when the dragon is more disguised. The hidden dragons are well camouflaged, so much so that often we don't see which parent is our real dragon.

*   *   *   *

The parent that we are sure we have the issues with is often not that one.

*   *   *   *

The saint-sinner syndrome occurs when we are determined to overvalue one parent and to undervalue another. As long as we see one parent as saint and the other as sinner, madonna or whore, king or bum, there is a corresponding imbalance within ourselves. And because we can not see our parents clearly, we will not be able to see our partners clearly either.

Mother, Is It You?

At an *Emerging Woman Seminar* in London, Margaret assumed that her major conflict was with her alcoholic and abusive father. He was the obvious dragon.

During the course of the weekend, she realized that her major issue was not with her father but with her mother. It was with the mother that she had her deepest and most buried feelings of distrust! She resented her mom for not protecting her from her father.

As Margaret continued exploring her feelings, she confronted an alarming truth. Like her mother, she could not stand up for herself. She failed to be firm and clear. She avoided taking positive steps or being direct to meet unpleasant situations. She, too, was afraid of losing the love of those she held dear. In many ways, she was just like her mother!

As she began to understand herself, Margaret could better understand her mother. Compassion replaced recrimination. Margaret gained a new sense of self-worth and the potential for new directions in her life. She had unearthed the gold that could enrich her life.

During a ceremony, Margaret forgave her mother, releasing her from further blame. As her final step, Margaret pledged to let go of her need to please others at the cost of her own integrity. In the future, she would empower herself through right action.

Sandra's Story

Sandra's father was overbearing, difficult, angry, and authoritarian. His communications were direct and forceful. At the dinner table she remembers being told in abusive language, "Shut up and eat your dinner." Sandra avoided problems with her father by imitating her mother's behavior: being quiet and staying out of his way. Mother was mild-mannered, non-confrontational. She did everything nice for her family. In her quiet way, though, she made it obvious she was a Suffering Martyr. To Sandra, mother was the saint and daddy was the sinner.

When Sandra married, she re-enacted the same patterns as her mother, playing the nice, sweet, Pleasing Passive to an overbearing, angry male. After many years, her husband walked out on her. Sandra was bitter about men. Self-righteous about her plight, she wondered why she had to suffer so much and why her life was so difficult. The martyr pattern was deeply ingrained.

Sandra was in no hurry to replace her husband. The years passed and she was comfortable in a nurturing role with men and chose to keep her relationships on a friendship-only basis. A deep interest in spirituality, religion, and philosophical concepts filled the void for her. Her energy went to the Father God.

In her fifties, life presented Sandra with a difficult challenge. Her ailing mother came to live with her. She was bedridden and required constant care. The tension and stress of dealing with her mother's nursing care and confinement began to take its toll on Sandra. Working all day at a full-time job and then coming home to another full-time commitment was wearing physically and emotionally. Meanwhile, her mother was riddled with pain and often overcome with depression.

"Can you turn me again? Is there something else to eat other than this? I need something else to drink. The light is too bright. Turn it down." The needs seemed endless. Sandra's attitude toward her mother changed. She no longer saw her as the saint; she wearied of her complaints. Much to her surprise, Sandra found herself responding to her mother in a style very similar to that of the father. There *was* some redeeming quality to his insistence on directness. What a revelation! Sandra discovered she had to set limits for her own time and for what she could and could not do, even though she may want to, for her mother. She was forced to develop the positive male within herself. Her challenge was to communicate with the directness of the father but to avoid the harsh negative tone.

Now that Sandra sees the value of her father, she is less inhibited, more open and honest in her communications. She can stop being a Suffering Martyr and a Pleasing Passive. And her mother has to come off her pedestal. Though Mom nurtured well, she wasn't direct and didn't know how to stand up for herself.

Often we discover, as did Sandra, that our greatest strength comes once we understand the parent with whom we had our greatest challenge! As Sandra grows in appreciating the value of both, not just one parent, she grows more in balance within herself.

Healing the Dragon Fight

When I lay on that grassy bank as a little child, wondering why I had been born in *that* family, I was sure that the real dragon to fight was my mother. But many years later, an incident occurred which jolted me into a new awareness.

It was when David, my older son, was just a toddler. I took him home to Front Royal to visit. One evening, my mother offered to put David to bed. From the next room, I could hear her singing a lullaby. The words, the cadences, the inflections were identical to the way I sang the same song. The same caring and tenderness I felt for little David was in her voice. How could I ever have thought we were so unlike each other? How could I have overlooked this part of her?

I had always appreciated Mother's enormous strength, independence and individuality. Somehow, I wasn't willing to value her softness and her maternal nature. Acknowledging that part of her helped me end my dragon fight.

The truth is we can end the Dragon Fight anytime we want. It requires only three things:

1. We must accept that our parents were not perfect people, but they were the perfect parents for us. They gave us the exact challenges we needed to become whole women.

2. We must give our parents back to our parents. Let them be who they are. They can never be real people as long as we hold on to our ideas, beliefs, and opinions about who or how we want them to be, or how they should be, or could have been. When we can accept them as they are, they no longer have to be the way we want them to be. We are then both free!

3. We must take responsibility for parenting and loving ourselves. Whatever our parents didn't do for us, we have to do for ourselves. It is that simple.

No More Tears

Leslie was a forty-year-old woman who came for counseling. Her outer appearance reflected her inner condition. Her clothes were colorless and drab, thrown together in a disheveled manner.

Leslie's mother had died when she was three. That had created a vacuum in her life that nothing seemed to fill. Thirty-seven years later, she was still grieving the loss of her mother. Her father had married soon after her mother's death. The treatment by the stepmother only reinforced Leslie's view of herself as an orphan, abandoned and unloved. Leslie experienced her stepmother as harsh and uncaring and faulted her for the lack of nurturing in her early life.

At that time, I sometimes included therapeutic massage in my sessions. Leslie was on the massage table, and as the session came to a close, I felt a sudden impulse to wrap her in a blanket in a particular way. As I folded the cover around her, I said, quite spontaneously, " No more tears, Leslie. No more tears." The words seemed to come from some other place. Tears began flooding down her face. My spontaneous gesture of empathy and caring connected Leslie with a memory of her mother tucking her in bed in similar fashion.

She shook with a powerful release of pent-up emotion. She wailed and sobbed as feelings of loss and sadness came spilling out from the depths of her being, At last, she sighed a sigh of completion. It was finished. It was time now for living.

In subsequent sessions, Leslie released more of her pain and accepted the responsibility for parenting herself. She began to pamper and nurture herself as she had yearned for her mother to do. She became her own loving mother, valuing her thoughts and feelings. She started to love her body and pay attention to her appearance. She indulged herself in long, hot soaking baths and had massages. For the first time in her life, shopping for attractive clothes for herself was fun, not a chore. Her inner metamorphosis was complete when, at a party, a young man told her, "You are a striking and beautiful woman." This was confirmation that what she was beginning to feel on the inside was visible on the outside.

Cold, Rigid and Dressed In Black

When I met Lynn, she was preparing to die. She was an attractive thirty-five-year-old woman, with a wonderfully supportive husband and three children. She was dying from cancer. Two years before she had had a mastectomy and the metastasis had spread throughout her body. In the face of death, Lynn's attitude was unusually positive. She had carefully put her life in order, assuring as smooth a transition for herself and her family as possible. She faced the prognosis with great courage.

When our counseling sessions began, there was only one thing left unfinished—her relationship with her mother—and that concerned her deeply. As our sessions unfolded, I could hardly believe that a woman such as the one Lynn described actually existed. When I met her mother, however, the description seemed completely accurate. Her mother was indeed cold, rigid, and severe. There was absolutely no touching, no show of feeling of any kind. She stood silently in the hospital room in her long black coat with her hair chopped ragged and close to her head. It was difficult to imagine her in a maternal role. She seemed more like a grim prison warden.

In one session, Lynn remembered a painful childhood experience that was so humiliating and traumatic that it literally chilled me as she relived it.

"I was six years old," she said. "I had a new dress on, and I got it wet. I was playing by the stream, and I wasn't supposed to play there. When my mother found me there, she began screaming and yelling about the dress—and what a bad girl I was!" Lynn paused and took a deep breath. It was obvious the pain of this experience was deep.

"Then she started to yank and pull me. The next thing I knew she had a rope. She was still yelling and shouting at me about ruining the dress. And then she pushed me against a tree and tied me to it." Lynn bit her lip and tried to hold back her tears. She started to sob.

"And she left me there," she said. I could hear the frightened child in her voice, still trembling, bewildered, and alone.

The painful memories had to be healed. So much of herself was invested in those early wounds. Whatever part of us that is caught in the past cannot live in the present.

The next day, I took Lynn through a guided visualization experience to help heal those early childhood memories. It was important to re-enter that experience and transform it.

She lay quietly before me. Her eyes were closed, and she was breathing rhythmically while soft, soothing music played in the background. I gave a suggestion to go back in time, to when she was six years old.

Lynn found herself tied to the tree again, feeling alone and terrified.

"Is there anyone there to help you?" I asked.

She paused. "Yes," she murmured, "I see someone. It is Jesus." her voice was calm and even. "Jesus is coming down the path to help me." Lynn was a woman of great faith, and I knew, from other conversations, that Jesus was someone she totally trusted.

"What is He doing now?" I asked.

"He is walking toward me." She smiled. "And now he is untying the rope. There, now, the rope is gone."

"What do you feel now?"

"I'm not afraid anymore. There is so much love." Suddenly, her face relaxed totally and she was silent.

I stopped, careful not to intrude upon this moment, allowing the inner experience to unfold. Her face tensed slightly.

"What is happening now?"

"I see my mother. She's dressed in black. She looks angry. I feel afraid."

"Don't stop now, Lynn. Go on. What's happening now?"

"Jesus has me by the hand, and we're walking toward my mother. I'm not afraid. My mother seems different now. She is looking at me warmly. Now we're standing together in a circle. We're all holding hands. My mother is smiling."

Lynn grew silent again, her inner gaze fixed upon that scene of love and reconciliation. She opened her eyes and smiled.

"My mother didn't know how to be a mother." There wasn't a trace of criticism, pain, or judgment in her voice. "When we were standing in the circle, holding hands with Jesus, I could feel how scared and frustrated being a parent made her. It was something she never understood."

For the next few days, Lynn practiced visualizing a reconciliation with her mother. She had healed the past, and now she wanted to heal the present. In her mind, she saw herself sitting in her rocking chair in a front room and her mother coming toward her, and both of them embracing. She practiced this visualization over and over again until it became a living experience.

Two weeks after the guided imagery session, she and her mother were reconciled. "For the first time in my life, my mother actually reached out and hugged me," Lynx told me. "She even shed tears. In fact, we both cried together."

Four months later, Lynn died in her sleep, in peace. She was a powerful teacher for me.

Fears to Pass Through: The Death of My Father

My father was eighty-five years old when he died of cancer. All his life he had been an energetic, positive, vibrant man. His diagnosis was not easy for him. But the same humor, iron will, and absolute honesty with which he had always approached life stayed with him during his illness.

Several months before he died, I had a short but vivid dream that awakened me in the middle of the night. In the dream, my father was scratching his skin and pulling his hair.

In real life, my father had little hair. He had been bald as long as I could remember. The dream had a symbolic message. My father (my male side) was disturbed. Scratching skin indicated things bothering me (getting under my skin), and the hair-pulling was thoughts I wanted to release. Dreams are first and foremost about the self. I had the sense, though, that there were things my father wanted to release as well. It was an intense dream; it seemed an urgent call for help. The next morning, I canceled all my appointments and made the five-hour drive back to Front Royal.

Five hours is a long time to drive, and I did some serious soul-searching along the way. My father was the parent I always wanted to emulate. He was warm, generous, and wise. And, although we didn't always agree, I valued his high ideals and integrity. His way of life was honorable and respectful. It was what I was striving for in my own way.

With my father, there were no secrets. He was frank, open,

and clear. And he was facing his illness, as he had his life, with directness and honesty. He had no illusions. He knew his cancer was terminal. He chose to spend his last days at home with his family and to die in his own bed.

I had no doubts about the bond between us. Our love for each other was strong and clear. But what wasn't clear was his understanding and acceptance of my divorce. The thought of his leaving without this sensitive issue being resolved was painful. I had talked with him about it, but there was a lot I hadn't shared with him, a lot I had left unsaid.

My father didn't believe in divorce. Marriages were forever, regardless. Although he was a staunch Baptist, to me he was like a wise and benevolent rabbi, a kind but firm man of the law. I knew he had suffered a great deal over my decision to divorce. Would he accept me as a divorced woman who chooses for herself, with her own reasons for dissolving the marriage bonds? I knew he wanted to understand my reasons. But it was difficult for me. It required me to voice things that were hard to say. If I couldn't be honest and he were to die with some misunderstanding, how would I feel? Or how would he feel? Could I trust myself to express my views confidently and directly, still valuing my decisions? Suppose he still didn't approve—even on his deathbed? Would I hold back and become the Pleasing Passive even now?

"Betty, be yourself." My father's counsel to me had always been wise and simple. "Be natural. Know your heart." Those words have always been a source of strength for me. In myths, the dragon slayer is the one who knows himself, trusts his own ability, and confronts the task—not by comparing his strength to the strength of the dragon, but by attuning himself to the power within. As I drove up to the house, my prayer was that I would be guided by love, not fear.

There were awkward moments at first. I was strained and overcautious. At times, I found myself falling into my familiar pattern of holding back. My deepest, heart-felt desire was to say all I needed to say, and I sensed I would never have an opportunity like this with my father again. Our love for one another was stronger than my fears. The nervousness quickly faded, and soon I began sharing intimately and fully.

We spent four days together. We laughed. We talked. We

cried. Many issues were healed during those hours together, both in my life and his. At times the parent-child role reversed. I was the mother and he, the son; I became the teacher and he, the student. I was no longer just a daughter, but a friend, a loved one—a whole person. Those days together were sacred space.

On the last day we were together, I sat in the room, watching him as he dozed. Suddenly, I felt the urge to go over and put my hands all over his face and that wonderful, shiny bald head. I stood there, touched to the core, pouring out all the deep love I had for him. He awoke, and with misty eyes and a smile, he looked up at me and said, "We really do love each other, don't we?" At the end of those four days, when I left my father, I knew he was at peace. And so was I.

The feelings had been deep, and there were moments of great sadness. But as I drove back to Virginia Beach, the sadness didn't touch me, not now. There was too much to be thankful for, too much to appreciate: the dream that had called me to him, the absolute clarity and conviction that had pressed me to go and be with him, and then the strength to speak from the heart. As father and daughter, and as soul to soul, we had experienced and explored new depths and intimacy with each other.

I was all I could be to him, and he had shared himself fully with me. It was a moment of Life, not death, for both of us.

A few days later, my mother telephoned to say my father's cancer had advanced. Any fleeting hope of a remission was gone. The cancer had spread all through his body. He last remaining strength was gone. He was now too weak to speak. Those wonderful, comforting words of this great man would be no more. I sat down and wept. The tears were bittersweet.

Yes, there had been fears to pass through. Both he and I were making transitions. The love and support we had given one another had prepared us both to step into that Unknown that lay ahead both in his life and in mine.

Healing the Relationship With Your Parents

(Allow 10-15 minutes or longer)
Begin by playing soothing, relaxing music. *Faerie Queene*, Side Two, is a suggestion. Lie down or sit with your spine erect.

Take a few breaths, breathing in peace, relaxation, and stillness. Breath out tension, stress, and negativity. Let your breathing be rhythmical and easy.

Reverie

Find yourself now in a meadow—move and feel the earth under your bare feet. Feel the texture of the grass as you walk. Become aware of the presence of life all around you, the sounds of animals, the songs of birds, the music of the breeze blowing gently through the trees, the splash of water in a nearby brook. It is twilight. Soft light slants across the meadow.

Move to a clearing in the meadow. Off to the side there is a clump of trees. As you stand there in the clearing, your mother and father step out from the trees. Look at them curiously.

Who are these people?

(Pause)

Now your mother steps forward. Be aware of the relationship you had with her. What was it like? Be aware of what you feel—not what you were supposed to feel. It doesn't matter that everybody says that you are supposed to love your mother. If you did, you did. And if you don't, you don't.

Do you love her? Do you not love her? Whatever you feel is all right.

What is it you want to say to her now? Say all those things you've never said. Communicate them non-verbally. If you need to forgive, forgive. If you need to be angry, be angry. If you want to tell her she did a good job, say so. Say all the things that you need to say.

(Long pause)

Now look closely at this women. Be aware of her humanness. Be aware that she was never trained to be your mother. Imagine what it was like for her to have you as her daughter. Look into her eyes and be aware that this woman did all she knew to do.

Understand as much as you can about her at this moment. Accept what you can. Ask yourself, what do I need to do to heal this relationship?

Now she steps back, and your father steps forward.

Be aware of the relationship you had with him. What was it like? Be aware of what you feel as he steps forward—not what you were supposed to feel. Do you love him? Do you not love him? Whatever you feel is all right. It doesn't matter that everybody says that you are supposed to love your father. If you did, you did. And if you don't you don't.

What is it you want to say to him right now? Say all those things you've never said. Communicate them non-verbally. If you need to forgive him, forgive. If you need to be angry, be angry. If you want to tell him he was great, tell him. Say all the things that you need to say. Experience it, and get finished with it.

(Pause)

Now look closely at this man. Be aware of his humanness. Be aware that he was never trained to be your father. Imagine what it was like for him to have you as his daughter. Look into his eyes and be aware that this man did all he knew to do.

Understand as much as you can about him at this moment. Accept what you can. Ask yourself, what do I need to do to heal this relationship?

(Pause)

Now he steps back and joins your mother. Watch them as they step back into the grove of trees.

Turn and leave the clearing. Walk across the meadow. Be aware that you can come to this meadow as often as you like to be with your parents.

Notice now that the day is nearly over. The last bit of light fades from the sky. Slowly bring the experience to a close.

Leave the meadow. Bring your attention back to your body and to the room you are in. Be with your feelings for a moment. . .start to stretch your body. . .breathe deeply. . .move. . .come back refreshed.

Note:

Write out your experience in a journal or discuss your feelings with your partner or support group. Sharing can reinforce the experience.

The reverie can be repeated as many times as is necessary until the relationship is healed.

Four Parent Picture Examples

The commentary on these four Parent Pictures will help you better assess your own drawing.

The Pleasing Passive

• Irene sees her mother as a little girl, a Pleasing Passive. Note the woman's feet pointing toward the man, the outstretched hand with the flowers, and the pubescent body (no curves, no bosom, no shape in the legs).

• The tight arms, chains, choker on the neck, and the "buttoned-up" front suggest that the woman feels imprisoned by her self-assigned role, but is determined to stay pleasing and pretty all the while.

• The father appears youthful and immature. The broad shoulders, thick arms, and heavy hands suggest a lot of power. Notice the thick belt over an out-of-proportion groin area—strong sexual energy and a difficult task in controlling it. His feet are pointing away from the female, indicating his direction is away from her, and she is in pursuit of him.

• As a result of her early conditioning, Irene, like so many women, is unsure about male energy. When men are dominating, angry, forceful, she confuses that with power because it gets results. She identifies with the mother and is overwhelmed when this assertive, forceful male energy is directed at her. Irene has a lot of underlying terror about men and her inability to stand up to them and to express herself. To "keep things nice," she stays a Pleasing Passive, not a mature, real woman.

• As long as she looks outside of herself, to the men in her life, for approval, she will never have it. What she is reaching out for so desperately in the picture is her own positive male self.

The Stronger Of The Two

• So much about Vivian's perception of her parents is communicated just by the placement of the figures on the page. The father is turned, giving a side view, and the mother's gaze is turned away from him.

• Certainly, Vivian considers her mother the stronger of the two. She has inner serenity, an inner confidence, and graceful beauty that makes her a most compelling woman. She appears self-contained as though she has neither the need nor the desire for the man to fulfill her. Though the copy of the drawing is only in black and white, in the original drawing, the mother is arrayed in beautiful and harmonious colors, symbolizing the colorful and interesting nature of this woman. She is no doubt artistic, with a keen aesthetic sense.

• On the other hand, the father is drawn in weak, vague, nondescript colors. Vivian perceives him as needing to be taken care of by the stronger woman. He is sensitive and soft, a "Peter Pan" or "flying boy." He has not cultivated his own sense of self-direction and waits for the woman to wake him up. The side-view, reflecting partial understanding, suggests Vivian does not know this man well.

• Vivian identifies with the mother. As an adult, her attractions and affection are directed toward women. She feels secure with women, particularly with older women who display the same inner strength that she so admired in her mother.

• The drawing indicates that Vivian wants to forget about her father and men in general. That is all the more reason she needs to deal with them. There may be an earlier incident that she is trying to blot out. It would be helpful to open and explore early memories and experiences with her father. Also, by developing male friendships (open communication, understanding, mutual respect), Vivian could learn to value men much more.

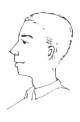

Everything In Its Place

• This picture could have been drawn by many individuals, especially those who had the similar pre-1950s family. In this scenario, which was common in that generation, the father was "higher" and the mother was "lower."

• Notice that carefully-drawn, clear line that the mother stands on and the father steps over. This is a traditional family structure and there is a sense of security in knowing that meals are regular, bedtime is a special ritual, daddy comes home for dinner, and there is always milk money in the school lunch box. Family is important and everyone and everything has its place. All works well as long as everyone agrees to this very defined structure.

• Jeanette's father is depicted as strong, reliable, responsible, capable. The pitchfork and shovel in his hand gives him a sense of a strong work ethic. There is a feeling that this man is direct and orderly. He is the strong one in the family and definitely wields the power. Notice that he is the only one in the picture with an open mouth, emphasizing that he is the voice for the family. The mother also fits the traditional role model of that time. She is nurturing, hard-working, and supportive. Notice that she stands on the line. She has positioned herself to stand securely in her place, careful not to cross over into the unknown.

• Jeanette places herself between the two parents, closer to the mother. The mother's hand rests gently on her shoulder. It would seem that she would tend to model herself after her mother and attempt to re-enact the same scenario in her marriage. Jeanette is slightly "off the line" but has not ventured forward yet. She, too, has work to do, as evidenced by the hoe. With the work ethic so strong, much of her value will be determined by what she does, not who she is.

• All appears in order, except for the heavy lines beneath the figures. This indicates there is a lot underneath that is not explored or dealt with. This might imply family secrets of one kind or another. There is a tight lid on things, and that lid is not to be taken off.

• Because of the setness in Jeanette's patterning, her tendency was to make life the way it should be rather than how it is. A major breakthrough for Jeanette came with a daughter who helped her move beyond rigid boundaries. Her daughter definitely did not fit the mold. During a rebellious period, she was sexually promiscuous and was a political activist. Jeanette was forced to change her perspective. She had to expand her view of life, to love enough to step across the line to reach her daughter.

The Jaded Eye

• When people draw only a face, and in this case with only one feature, the distorted view indicates how little the child knows the parent. Leah sees her father as a real "boogie man." She is in real fear of him.

• Her mother is drawn full-figured, but without a face. No identity. She is in the background, "waiting on the sidelines." The mother's arms have many lines, and she holds her hands together. This suggests an enormous amount of emotion and withheld feelings that she is afraid to express. The mother also has no feet. Her foundation as a woman is missing. She has lost her "footing." She is rendered powerless through her fear of her husband. Both Leah and her mother were subject to the violent outbursts of the father and felt inadequate to cope with his overpowering energy.

• In a situation where there is such a tremendous fear of male energy, and no real support from the mother, Leah was given little sense of self, little assurance that she was safe and secure. We look to our parents for physical and emotional safety. She had neither. She learned to be deceptive, to hide truth, to disguise feelings to get by and "make do," anything to survive. There is an underlying terror that if her "Real Self" is found out, she won't be acceptable. As an adult, authority figures will be challenging to Leah. She will want to give up her power or get out of the way to avoid conflict. She may go to great efforts to disguise or mask parts of herself. Once she accepts herself and her own inner authority, outer authority figures will no longer present a challenge.

• Before Leah can see the good in her father, or in men in general, she must deal with her fear of angry men and her hidden fear that if she lets her anger out, she will be just like her father. She needs to practice dealing with situations as they come up, rather than waiting for things to build up and get out of control. It is extremely important that Leah give herself permission to comment on what she sees, what she feels, what she believes, whether it is acknowledged or not. When she knows her own worth, she will have her "footing" as a woman.

Betrayal is the death of trust.

Betrayals happen whenever we feel
used, abandoned, rejected, or sacrificed.
Betrayals are the result of unclear
agreements or unrealized expectations.

In this chapter, you will learn
how you set yourself up for betrayal,
what is learned from these experiences,
and how to move beyond
betrayal to self-empowerment.

Love is expecting people to keep
their agreements.
Wisdom is knowing they won't,
always.
Self-love is loving yourself
even when they don't.

Chapter 3
Beyond Betrayal

I was six years old when my brother James was born. It was a thrilling event for me. I was no longer the youngest in the family! To me he was the most beautiful baby that had ever been born. His eyes were bright and laughing. His soft curls fell gently on the nape of his neck. And the smell of Johnson's Baby Powder that always surrounded him was a sweet incense that was intoxicating.

I became James's "little momma"—his ally and friend. James was a deep and sensitive child who always needed to be comforted in the presence of pain of any kind. I remember once when a bat flew down our chimney. It was thrashing around the living room, knocking things over. In desperation, my mother grabbed a broom and swatted and poked at it, trying to get it out of the house. James immediately burst into tears, afraid the bat might get hurt.

The same acute sensitivity was evident in our shared childhood adventures. James would be the one to discover the animal in need and then proceed to become the self-appointed doctor. And it was James who would insist on conducting proper funerals for any dead animal we discovered on the roads or in the fields.

Aware of his extra antennae, I always felt a need to nurture and protect him, to minimize the disappointments, to soften life somewhat. At Christmas, for example, I would always question my mother ahead of time about what she had bought for James. Then, if I felt the gifts were not appropriate or if she hadn't gotten him enough, I would badger her unmercifully until she bought more.

The empathetic bond continued throughout our growing-up years. As we matured, I dropped the caretaking role and our relationship shifted into a more balanced one of mutual support. As adults, James and I both became involved in a spiritual search at the same time. We would frequent the Association of Research and Enlightenment in Virginia Beach and study the Edgar Cayce readings together. I had first introduced James to the work of Edgar Cayce, and then he, in return, introduced me to Peter and the New Age Center, also at Virginia Beach. As we awakened to the life of the Spirit, we made a trip to Israel together to retrace the paths of early Christianity. Our hours were filled with excited conversation, philosophical discussions, laughter, and precious joy.

But, in time, "it" happened. I was recently divorced and on my own when James approached me about borrowing a fairly substantial sum of money. At the time, he was involved in several construction projects and wanted to keep his bank loan down to a minimum.

We had always been loving and supportive to each other. To me, the matter was simple. I had the money, and he needed it. I loaned him what I had, without any written agreement, signatures, or significant record-keeping. I was content to trust him and collect the monthly interest payments that we agreed upon. The arrangement worked fine—except that no buyers for the houses or apartments appeared. Before long, James's money ran out and my payments stopped.

James made sudden plans to move back to Israel, leaving the unsold buildings behind. Angry and alarmed, I confronted him the night before he left. I accused him. I blamed him. I attacked. Gentle, sensitive James couldn't handle my highly charged emotional state. This was a part of Betty he had never experienced. The nurturing, older sister had suddenly become a Shrieking War Goddess. Not knowing how to respond, he instinctively reacted with a self-defensive rage.

The next thing I knew he was pushing and shoving me out of his room. In my anger, I turned again toward him, but he fled the room. I followed after James to call him back. Unknown to him, I tripped and sent myself headlong into the wall. I felt my body thud and then I collapsed, unconscious.

When I woke up, there was no one to help me up. I was

stunned. Slowly, I got myself together and limped home, trembling, shaken, and confused. I went into the bathroom and began filling the tub with water. It was the only way I knew to nurture myself. I stepped out of my clothes and slipped into the soothing warmth of the water. And then the tears started to flow. I couldn't stop crying. All I had ever known from James was love. How could he do this? Abandon me! Desert me! Anger me! *Betray me!* The hours went by without a word. No phone call, no apology, no heroic commitment to help me out of the specter of debt and insecurity. That day, James left on his desperate exodus to Israel. I was left with the rubble of broken trust and a life turned upside down.

If this had been my only challenge, I could have handled it. But this was only the beginning. Within a year, every significant male relationship in my life would be wrenched away, challenging me to claim my own strength.

As a divorcee, I had long since ceased being Mrs. Prominent Attorney's Wife, circulating at country clubs and resting high on the guest list for the best parties. Now, instead of shopping at Bloomingdales, I was struggling to get credit at Sears. In addition, I found myself pitted against my ex-husband in a serious legal battle over real estate holdings.

I was convinced Sean wanted revenge and was taking out his hurt and frustration by using his legal training against me. He had skills, knowledge, and "the system" on his side. We had to deal with each issue, case by case, and the process was long and protracted. One property settlement alone went on for months. After many tense sessions with a mediator, plus three pre-court hearings, the case was settled out of court in my favor. But it was an empty victory. The strain of the constant challenge, accusations, and recriminations had worn me out. Until then, I had never had to stand up for myself. Now it seemed that the only thing I was doing was battling and struggling just to survive.

At this same low period, my father died of cancer. He had suffered a long time, and I had watched the disease gradually eat away his body. I felt such empathy for him that I started to develop pre-cancerous conditions myself. Somehow, I had developed an unconscious belief that I could help my father by taking on his illness. It was a heroic fantasy born from a feeling of powerlessness to help one whom I dearly loved. The belief was totally irrational. It took hard work to turn this self-sabotaging belief around and restore my health.

When my father died, the feeling of loss was tremendous. My father loved me unconditionally. I grew up with the secure feeling that he would always be there when I needed him. Suddenly, there was a void. No open arms. No reassuring voice. Gone were the strength and the wisdom that counseled me. He was dead, and I was unprotected.

About this same time, my fourteen-year-old son John, who was living with me, made a sudden decision to go back and live with his father. He was unhappy with the public school in our neighborhood. He wanted to return to the same private school he had attended before the divorce. So John left, and my heart sank.

As my financial crisis worsened, I turned to my older brother, John, for help. It took all my courage to pick up the phone. I had to be desperate before I could admit I needed help. I had never done it before. His response was chilling. "I'm sorry, Betty, but my money is all tied up. I can't help you now." John was being honest and clear. But to my vulnerable ears it seemed cold, impersonal. My mind flashed back to warm memories of our happy childhood games and the pride and comfort I had always felt in having him as my brother. But that was then. At this moment I felt a judgment behind his words. I had made a bad money decision with James. I had made my own choice to divorce. I would have to live with those results. How different everything seemed now that I was single.

If I had had the courage to confess to John how truly desperate I was, his response would, no doubt, have been different. He had always seen me as confident and capable. In his opinion, my situation might be uncomfortable, but it was nothing to get overly excited about. He was certain I could handle it. I was too stuck in my pride to speak out. The harsh truth was I was definitely on my own.

My husband, my father, my son, my brothers, all the significant male relationships of my past, relationships that had helped define who I was, that had given me a sense of security and purpose, were crumbling away. They were ruptured and broken by pressures and challenges I had never known before.

It was a painful transition time. Yet, it was an exciting time, as well. There were fresh ideas and new relationships that helped me explore other sides of myself that I had only glimpsed previously. Three people, in particular, played significant roles during this transitional time. One of them, Francis, was fiery and impulsive. He had a passion for frank, honest communication and a commitment to truth. Through him, I began to discover the challenges, the risks, and the beauty of relating in total honesty. I learned what it was to share feelings, thoughts, emotions, fears, and uncertainties. With him, there could be no sham, no games, no masks. Here was the possibility for real growth. And then suddenly, with little warning, he moved back to Pennsylvania.

Peter was a spiritual mentor and beloved friend. He, more than anyone, stirred deep memories at a soul level. He rekindled an idealism and desire for service that had long been dormant. Peter's wise counsel, humor, and insight helped me through many troubles and blind spots. He was the first to encourage me to teach. With his encouragement I begin to speak to groups about dreams, meditation, and personal transformation. When he sensed I could do this on my own, he pushed me from the nest. As he withdrew, my feeling of loss was as great as the bond I had felt with him was strong.

Then there was Jason, the imaginative, fun-loving mystic. With Jason, I considered the possibility of a lifelong relationship. In time, though, our differences became too great, our philosophies too divergent, and the dream ended.

Throughout this bizarre chain of reversals and unmet expectations, I was being continually thrown back on myself and myself alone. In countless ways, I felt betrayed. There had been too much loss in too little time.

What is Betrayal?

Betrayal is the death of trust.

At some time in our lives, most women feel they have been betrayed. Betrayals happen whenever we feel used, abandoned, rejected, or sacrificed.

A betrayal experience can be just as devastating as losing a loved one through death. The same grief and sorrow is there. There seems to be no outlet for the feelings of loss, no source of comfort, no end to the pain.

Our betrayals usually come through someone we love the most—a father who leaves us, a mother who belittles us, a husband who decides that we are no longer exciting, a girlfriend who goes after our man. But there is never a hurt that can't be overcome. And there is never a hurt, beyond the first moment, that is not self-inflicted. Hurts are real. They can be engendered by other people, but they can be sustained only by us.

The power comes by knowing that no matter what happens to me, I can overcome it. I can turn it around and transform it. Nothing can stop me from being my own fulfilled person. No other person, no matter how they abuse me, can strip me of my rights or rob me of my self-esteem. How I experience myself is my decision.

Love is expecting people to keep their agreements.
Wisdom is knowing that sometimes they won't.
Self-love is loving yourself, even when they don't.

How Betrayals Happen

Most betrayals are innocent. We seldom set out to hurt or be hurt by someone. Betrayals are the result of unspoken or unclear agreements, and betrayals are the result of unrealized or unrealistic expectations.

Innocent Betrayals

When we are children, betrayals usually come from our parents or other important authority figures, making their impact all the more devastating. Often, the adults involved are unaware that the situation is in any way troublesome. The young child feels overwhelmed, unable to express feelings, and begins to expect life to be full of disappointments. And the hurt gets buried, often surfacing years later in some disguised manner.

Alice, a client, remembers being sick with consistent sore throats as a child,. The doctors recommended a tonsillectomy. Her parents assured her that having her tonsils out would be quite an adventure. They told her stories about how nice the doctors and nurses would be, how they would take care of her and even give her vanilla ice cream, which was her favorite flavor.

Alice remembers walking down the sidewalk toward the hospital, firmly holding the hands of both parents and gazing confidently up at the faces of these two people she trusted so completely.

The first evening in the hospital was just as she anticipated: kind doctors and caring nurses taking special care of her. Even the promised ice cream was hers for the asking. The next morning, though, was an experience in terror. She awakened from the operation with excruciating pain. Her throat felt mutilated and raw. Startled and terrified, she tried to call for help, but no words came out. She looked for her parents, but they were gone. Her father had gone to work, and her mother had stepped out to eat at the hospital cafeteria. There were no doctors in sight and the nurses were busy elsewhere. There was no comfort or explanation about what had happened. She felt totally alone and abandoned. Something deep inside died that day. Her throat has long since healed, but Alice is still in pain. Learning to trust is still a big issue in her life.

Most of us can remember at least one "innocent betrayal" from our childhood. When I was a little girl, I remember being fascinated with a new box of payons (a type of special crayon/paint) that my sister Joanna got when she began the third grade. The colors and the texture of the payons were different than anything I owned. I asked my mother if I could have a box like Joanna's. "Sure," she replied. "When you get to the third grade, you can have a box, too."

I remembered that promise, and I thought about it often as I fantasized the drawings and designs I would make. When I started the third grade, two years later, I asked my mother excitedly, "Now can I have my payons?"

She had already bought all my school supplies and had no idea of the urgency behind my request. Her reply was very matter-of-fact: "You don't need anything else now."

I had waited two years, never doubting her promise. I felt betrayed.

Unspoken Agreements

Betrayals can result when unspoken agreements are not clarified. The underlying belief is that the other person should somehow know what we expect. The following incident is the result of not bothering to verbalize an agreement.

Linda is strongly attracted to Ron and decides to become sexually involved. They spend the night together. In the morning, Linda immediately starts talking about what they will do that evening and how they can spend the upcoming weekend together. Ron starts to feel nervous. He is forthright and tells her that he is sorry that she has built expectations. The truth is that he is just not a one-woman man. Or he may be deceptive, make excuses, and just not show up again. Either way, she feels betrayed. He did not fulfill her unspoken agreement.

Unclear Agreements

When we've made an agreement with a close friend, a lover, child, or partner, and these agreements are broken, the deepest wounds are made.

We are most vulnerable in our personal relationships.

Even when we have made what we believe to be clear agreements, we may have different understandings about what words mean.

In *Annie, Get Your Gun*, a comic operetta popular a few years ago, there was a humorous but poignant scene that illustrates this point. The hero, a handsome young tenderfoot from the East, is smitten by Annie, a gun-toting, outspoken, independent woman of the Wild West. Finally, he summons up his courage and asks her to marry him. She joyously agrees. Then in a melodious duet, she, on one side of the stage, sings of long gowns, fancy parties, and life in the city. He, on the opposite side of the stage, sings of his longing for log cabins, home-spun cloth, and life in the wild. Betrayal is inevitable.

Unrealized Expectations

When we don't know ourselves, we don't know our partners. We don't relate to real people, but to our image of how we want them to be, how we need them to be; and we agonize when they don't measure up. The inevitable occurs when our expectations are not met. Always trust people and trust people to be who they are!

Harriet is a divorced woman who feels she needs a man. She begins a relationship with an aspiring lawyer, and all seems to go well. Soon he moves in with her and her two children, and the relationship continues for two years. Her expectation is that he will want the committed relationship and marriage that she wants. Ed is seven years younger than Harriet. When they talk about marriage, he becomes vague. After four years of being together, Harriet turns forty. Suddenly, Ed begins talking about how he would really like to have children and that she is too old. Harriet feels it is an excuse and not the real reason for breaking off the relationship. She senses he doesn't want marriage, period. The relationship ends. She feels betrayed.

Ed is content with compatibility. There is nothing in his history that indicates he would commit to marriage and a family. Each of his previous relationships have ended after four or five years. When marriage becomes the ultimate requirement, he bows out. Harriet is in love with the image of who she wants him to be, not who he is.

Moving Beyond Betrayal

One of the best metaphors on betrayal is in the fairy tale *The Girl with the Silver Hands*. There are many versions of this tale. This is the one I like to tell:

There was once a sea captain who lost a valuable treasure chest during a voyage. The Evil One, seeing his misfortune as an opportunity to capture a soul, made a deal with the Captain. He would restore the Captain's treasure if, in exchange, the Captain would give him the first thing he saw when he walked up the path to his home. The Captain accepted willingly.

The first thing he always would see when he walked the familiar path near his home was an apple tree by the gate. This would be a small price to pledge for the return of his treasure. For the rest of the voyage, there was fair wind and full sails. Laden with treasure, the Captain soon forgot his promise.

On his return, as he walked the familiar road to his house, his beautiful daughter—the "apple of his eye"—rushed to him with outstretched arms. His daughter, not the tree, was the first thing he saw. Through his greed, or limited vision, he had inadvertently betrayed his daughter.

The Captain, with tears in his eyes and an aching heart, remembered his pledge to the devil. But it was too late to change his bargain. That night, the daughter discovered her father's secret. She was horrified! Her horror turned to resignation and then to anger. To spite the devil and punish her father for his foolish vow, she cut off her hands and sent them in a box to the Evil One.

She ran away from home, fleeing from the father and all he represented. Angels guided her to a beautiful garden, where she could live in safety. Without hands, though, she had no way to feed herself. The angels whispered that she must stand on her toes to eat the berries and fruits that hung abundantly above her head.

She lived in her garden undisturbed, until one day a King discovered the garden and fell in love with her. Seeing that she had no hands, he commanded his royal silversmith to fashion silver hands for her. She became pregnant with his child. Before she could tell him the news, he left abruptly to go fight a war in a foreign country.

Meanwhile, the Evil One was enraged at being cheated out of his prize. With the King gone, the Evil One entered into an alliance with the Queen Mother. He spread vicious rumors about the girl with the silver hands in an effort to turn the kingdom against her. She was forced to flee again and go yet deeper into the wilderness. She gave birth to her child, whom she named Sorrowful.

Weak with thirst, she discovered an abandoned well, a deep source of spiritual nourishment and life. A mysterious and powerful voice, speaking from deep within the well, told her to put her hands in the water.

"I have no hands," she protested.

Again the voice urged, "Put your hands in the water."

This time she did. Magic happened. She felt a tremendous release from her sorrow and pain. When she withdrew her hands from the water, she discovered they were whole and real again.

Symbolically, her hands represent her power. When she severs her hands, she cuts herself off from her own power and gives it over to the dark force, the hidden or unconscious part of the self. Consciously and unconsciously, many women cut themselves off from their own power after a betrayal.

Even when we give away our power, in our deepest hurts and wounds, there is a way to feed and nourish ourselves. We must listen to our guidance. In fairy tales, myths, and folklore, guidance comes through angels or animals or nature itself. They provide answers and show the way out of impossible situations. In metaphor, they represent the higher aspect of self.

The woman who willfully cuts off her hands in reaction to the unintentional but thoughtless action of her father regains her strength by following the voice that comes from a deep, nourishing, but abandoned place. By dipping her wounds into the very source of life, the depths of her spirit, all that was lost is restored to her.

This story affirms for women that no matter how horrendous the experience has been, no matter how much trauma, sadness, or grief there has been, there is a time when it must end. The end comes when we, like the girl with the silver hands, are willing to put our hands in the water. To "put our hands in the water" is another way of saying that we must get in touch with our own deep feelings and move through them. We need to accept the sorrow, release the rage, shed the tears, and then reclaim our power. And we must do it alone. Though we can be helped along the way, no one ultimately can do it for us.

We end sorrow and claim life when we begin to trust that deep inner voice that speaks from our own depths. It re-empowers us and urges us to move on with our lives.

The year when I experienced so many betrayals was one of pure tragedy. My feelings of self-worth were low. I had created a drama, scene by scene, where I invited every significant male in my life to dismiss me, to put me out of their lives in one way or another.

On another level, the drama served a much greater purpose. All my life I had many males to support me, to care for, acknowledge, and encourage me. Because of that, the greater part of my inner strength lay dormant. Through the dramatic series of events, I was invoking some powerful challenges— "mythic tasks." With no powerful male to offer security or wisdom, I was forced to "put my hands in the water." In so doing life was asking to have the courage to trust my own truth.

We create the world we live in, giving people very specific communications about how they are to treat us. If we have low self-esteem, for example, we will give out that communication, and people will respond on cue to the roles we have chosen to play. Betrayal begets betrayal. Once betrayed, we continue the pattern. When we can change ourselves, we automatically will change the way we allow others to treat us.

When I could love myself again, I rewrote the script. My relationships began to re-form. Instead of tragic melodrama, I began creating an adventure, with romance, humor, joy, and personal fulfillment.

It is hard to let go of betrayal. It is harder not to.

Sharing the Gold of My Betrayal

One of the most humbling things about writing this book was to learn that "I" was not writing it. From the beginning, it seemed as if the book had a life of its own, and that a Higher Force, a consciousness different from my own, was directing it. Throughout the entire writing process, synchronistic events and situations would appear, as if on cue. Those timely events would present themselves in a manner that would force me to deal with the very thing I was writing about. The experience was highly personal and most confrontative. It was almost as if something were saying, "You are not going to write about theories or just other people's experiences—every lesson is yours!"

While organizing the Betrayal chapter, I was closeted off in a small room in the foothills of the Blue Ridge Mountains of Virginia. During that time alone, I was able to confront the hurts that I had been carrying within for several years but had so conveniently stuffed. Those periods when we are able to inter-face with ourselves at a profound level are sacred. They can not be forced. When the time is right, the memories, feelings, and insights bubble up into the conscious realm quite naturally.

During those three days alone, my tears could not stop flowing. It was as though I had started to unravel an endless cord with knots, one knot connected to another, each one with unexpressed feelings and unfinished business. One by one I pulled them out; feelings were so interconnected that it was difficult to know where one began and another ended. When the feeling of loss became too overwhelming, I would take warm baths, once at four in the morning. The warmth of the water was a source of calm and solace. There was the sense of being held in the womb of the Great Mother.

One thing was clear. It was up to me to heal the pain of my betrayals. The wound that was the deepest was the one with James, my brother. I had lived with the pain for three years, hanging on to my belief that I was "right" about how he had "wronged" me.

On the third night, I was awakened abruptly with a message running through my mind, "No one else can betray you. You can only betray yourself." It was as if this realization had been gestating deep within my own unconscious for some time, and now its time had come. It was truth that went beyond any intellectual or philosophical concept. It was a deep, penetrating, uncompromising experience of pure knowing. The only betrayal that is real occurs when we betray ourselves by allowing some person or situation to separate us from our real nature, which is Love!

By remaining righteously indignant and rationalizing my position, I had cut myself off from James. I needed to stop looking at what James did to me and look instead at what I was doing to myself. Instead of being immobilized in the hurt and pain of the past, I began to search instead for the beliefs, the programming, the conditioning, and the patterns of the past that were operating on an unconscious level and had attracted this experience.

When James approached me about borrowing money, I wanted to keep "everything nice." I avoided taking a stand. I avoided direct communication and did not insist on clarity. As a result, our agreements were not clear. I had gone into an emotional fog, naively hoping that everything would work out all right. But underneath the Pleasing Passive exterior was an imbedded, underlying terror of being responsible for myself. My unvoiced fear was that I couldn't handle my situation alone. I would sacrifice anything, including myself and my money, to keep others loving me.

To realize something is one thing; to take action is another. In order to own the truth, I needed to do something tangible. That morning I wrote a letter to James. I acknowledged my part in our three-year scenario. I told the truth: I was hurting. I loved him and our separation was painful. Holding back love always is. I wanted to drop the whole incident and no longer hold him responsible or accountable for the past.

It had been several years since I had seen James. The last time had been on Thanksgiving Day. We had sat awkwardly at separate tables and had exchanged only a few polite comments. This time when I saw James, it was at another family function. His eyes twinkled, and he grinned and hugged me warmly. That one moment was worth everything. The past was behind us. We could be loving once again. I had come home to my true self.

A friend shared a catharsis she experienced at the Wailing Wall in Jerusalem. Through the ages, many devotees have come to offer prayers. The prayers are written on small pieces of paper and ceremoniously placed in the cracks in the wall. Rachel's prayer was for the release of her grief. As she placed her prayer between two ancient bricks, she was suddenly overwhelmed with emotion and cried out, "I don't want to wail anymore." Tears began to flow. The burden and pain from forty years of blaming loved ones for her disappointments and despair was lifted.

Like Rachel, many women are seduced by the bittersweet melancholy of acting out the role of the "wronged woman."

Sadness is seductive. The more intense the suffering, the more the entrapment. Like the Girl with the Silver Hands, or Rachel at the Wailing Wall, we must face our sorrow. Once we acknowledge both the part we played in the experience and what we learned from the experience, we emerge as wiser women.

The Flying Boy

Helen had felt betrayed by men over and over again. The first step for her was to recognized that all the men she chose were just like her father.

Her father was the proverbial Peter Pan, a little boy that never grows up . He was a "flying boy," to use a modern day term. Her father was never there when she needed him. Flighty and irresponsible, this type of man is in constant need of mothering. He is out of touch with his own maleness and incapable of commitment and long-term relationships. These qualities described every male relationship she had ever had.

Once Helen saw the pattern, she could forgive her father for not being what she wanted in a father. She gave up her expectations of wanting him to be different than who he is. She could accept him as he is. The most important shift is that her attention is now on her life and the creation of a healthy male-female relationship rather than on the limitations of her father.

Daddy's Little Princess

Sarah tearfully shared how, as a little girl, she had always been Daddy's little princess. As she became older, her father seemed to suddenly turn on her. Instead of the warm praise and attention she had been accustomed to, she was accused of being sexually promiscuous, even before she knew the meaning of the term! She couldn't understand his change of heart. She was outraged and felt betrayed by his name-calling and innuendos.

In re-telling her story, Sarah realized that her father had been drawn to her sexually in her adolescence. His sexual urges toward his pubescent daughter confused him. He repressed those unacceptable feelings and projected his guilt on her.

Sarah began to understand that her father's emotional confusion had nothing to do with her worth as a woman. Once her own confusion cleared, she could forgive her father his frailties and gain back her own self-esteem.

Cold-Hearted Father

Annika, a young Dutch girl, wanted to confront her deep resentment toward her father. She described him as an intellectual who spent most of his time in his study. He was a person seemingly devoid of love or joy. He was neither affectionate nor emotionally supportive.

Annika was shocked to realize that she had developed a pattern similar to his. By blaming her father for his emotional deprivation, she cut herself off from her own power to create the joy and love she needs for herself.

If our loved ones don't, or can't, give us what we need, then we must give it to ourselves. It doesn't help to blame someone for being who they are. Annika's father gave her all the love he was capable of giving. It was the best he knew. The fact that it wasn't sufficient for her needs is not the issue now. What matters is that Annika realizes how much pain she has perpetrated on herself by wanting her father to be different.

Experiential Exercises For Moving Beyond Betrayal

Exercise One: A Letter To My Self

(To be done alone)

In the very center of each of us there is a source of life, an inner self, which knows exactly what we need at any given moment. The single most important thing we can do in life is to get in touch with this, our spiritual center.

The following exercise is designed to help communicate with your inner self. This can be a very useful in healing the deep pain of betrayal.

It is best to allow a whole evening for this exercise. Eliminate all outside distractions. Make your space private and sacred.

All you need is a pen and paper. You are going to write a letter to your inner self. Begin the letter "Dear Inner Self" or "Dear Teacher" or use whatever name invokes trust, love, empathy, compassion, wisdom, or understanding for you (Spirit, Soul, Christ, Master, etc). Assume that your inner teacher loves you more than you love yourself and has no need to judge or criticize you for whatever you have done, no matter what it is. You are free to express any and all feelings.

Take time to get in touch with the experience that carries the most pain for you. You may need to look at old photographs to evoke feelings and memories or to play a special song to carry you into the experience.

When you feel ready, begin to write freely and honestly about all your feelings surrounding that experience. Whatever was not said, say it now. Spend as long as it takes to get out all the emotions, feelings, and beliefs. Know that your inner self knows, accepts, and understands.

When you have completed your letter, ask yourself if you are ready to move beyond the pain. If you are, decide that this experience no longer has power over you and affirm that you are free of its impact or ability to influence your life.

Now look for the gold in that betrayal. What can you gain from it? Follow the steps outlined at the end of this chapter.

First, identify what you learned from the betrayal. Journaling helps clarify the experience.

Next, claim your gold powerfully!

Then, decide what action steps you need to take.

Exercise Two: Sharing and Listening

(To be done with a partner)

In this exercise, two friends agree to support each other in moving beyond betrayal. Arrange conditions which will insure uninterrupted time for this special sharing. Sit across from each other (cross-legged on the floor works well) with a lighted candle beside you.

Partner A begins by talking freely about a time in which she felt betrayed. She may need to talk briefly about several incidents until she uncovers the one with the most impact. The role of Partner B is to be the loving support person. Her role is to let her partner feel safe enough to freely share her inner self, Partner B listens only. This is not a time to give advice or opinions. If you are Partner B and your partner gets stuck, you may ask a leading question to help move her to clarity. For example, "How did you feel when that happened?" or "What was that experience like for you, when he said. . .?"

When Partner A has finished her story, the next step is to dismiss that experience from having any more power in her life.

Then dig for gold. The speaker identifies and affirms what she has gained from the betrayal. Again, Partner B is there to listen and to support her partner. You may assist by asking leading questions: "What beliefs do you want to change or let go of? What value has it had for you? How has the experience made you stronger, more sensitive, etc?"

When Partner A has finished, switch roles. The process begins all over again.

When both partners have completed the process, they take the candle in their hands (symbolizing the Light of Truth) and, holding it up together, lift the light above their heads while facing each other. Each partner takes turns forgiving the persons in their betrayal experience. Each states boldly the gold they have received from the betrayal and affirms their responsibility for creating their own joy!

When the shared light of understanding is held high, it is a powerful moment!

Love is expecting people to keep their agreements.
Wisdom is knowing that sometimes they won't.
Self-love is knowing you can handle it when they don't.

Guidelines For Moving Beyond Betrayal

1. Acknowledge Your Feelings

Talk out your feelings and emotions with an attentive, receptive partner. Until you feel that you have been really listened to, there can be no resolution. If there is no supportive partner available, write your feelings out in a journal.

2. Change Your Perspective

Understand the others involved in the situation. What were they thinking and feeling? What were their fears, expectations, assumptions? How did they experience the situation? Release and forgive! What expectations were not met? What agreements were not clear?

Your own belief systems helped create this situation. The other person was only an agent acting out your own reality. What are the beliefs that no longer serve?

3. Claim the Gold

The value is always there when you can understand your betrayal experience, not for the pain it produces but for the opportunity for healing and growth that it offers. Don't waste a good betrayal! Get the "gold" from it.

The following is some of the gold you may have gained from the betrayal experience.

Are you stronger, more compassionate, clearer about what you want or don't want in your life?

Decide to ask for what you want.

Decide to speak up sooner in the future when you don't agree.

Decide to stop agreeing just to get others' approval.

Decide to own your power, rather than give it away.

Decide to create supportive relationships in your life.

Decide to notice the truth of who he is rather than who you want him to be.

Decide to develop a stronger spiritual focus in your life and not make others responsible for your spirituality.

Decide to stop longing for unavailable relationships.

Decide to stop being *other*-identified and concentrate on *self.*

4. Follow-Through

Take positive steps to put your new understanding into practice. Real change requires a new response to an old

pattern. You may need to phone, write, or get with the person or persons by whom you felt betrayed in order to complete the process. Follow-through also includes making sure you have the support you need to make change permanent. (Support groups of various kinds are excellent for this.)

Visualization is a powerful tool for healing relationships and for changing negative patterns. Each day, relax for a few minutes, close your eyes, and focus on the person who betrayed you, seeing that person in a positive way (happy, smiling, laughing, singing, confident). Now see yourself at peace with that person.

See yourself the way you want to be.

You may need to repeat this exercise many times before you get results. But it works. Keep practicing! Continue as long as necessary.

* * * *

You know you have moved beyond betrayal when what you have learned from the experience equals or surpasses the amount of pain that you have invested in it.

The ability to transform life's
experiences is not new. It is part
of the ancient wisdom tradition which
belongs to many cultures. The Native American
tradition, in particular, shows a unique respect
and understanding of the feminine power found in
nature.
As women, we can learn to
tap the transformative power
of the elements fire, air, earth, and water.

Chapter 4
Practicing Your Magic

The Sweat Lodge Ceremony
and The Power of the Four Directions

A few years ago in Virginia Beach, I was invited to participate in a Native American Sweat Lodge Ceremony. I had no idea what a sweat lodge was, except that it was a traditional purification ceremony of the American Indian. I had great respect for the Native Americans' reverence for nature and was curious about their spiritual traditions, so I decided to experiment.

The ceremony began with a group of men and women sitting around a roaring fire. The shaman stood in the center, close to the fire, and began the ceremony by drawing deeply on his long-stemmed pipe and making an offering of smoke to each of the "grandfathers," the guardian spirits of the four directions. Then the group entered the sweat lodge, crawling on our hands and knees through the small opening in front of the fire. The lodge was a low dome built from bent saplings covered with black plastic and insulated by blankets and sleeping bags to hold in the heat. Inside, the lodge was pitch-black with only space enough to squat.

"This is the womb of Mother Earth," the shaman said, "which we enter in order to be reborn."

There was some nervous laughter and giggling as we entered and jostled and jiggled and squirmed in the darkness, squatting elbow-to-shoulder until we were all settled into place. The shaman was the last to enter and signaled for the first of the rocks to be brought in.

Seven rocks, heated to a red-hot intensity, were taken from the fire and placed in the pit in the center of the lodge. The flap was lowered, plunging us into total darkness except for the white glow of the rocks.

The sharp pungent odor of sage and cedar filled the lodge as the shaman threw sacred herbs on the rocks, followed by sputtering and sizzling as he began ladling water over the rocks. My eyes began to water from the smoke, and my skin felt seared by the sudden rise in temperature from the steam.

No one spoke, and the shaman began offering prayers to the grandfathers, invoking their presence in the lodge. My reactions were mixed. "Do I really have to sweat and bake in this heat to become spiritual?" I thought. I was dubious and resistant; and I felt curious rather than expectant.

"Are these people really into this?" I wondered with a feeling of ridicule. "Or are they just kidding?" Virginia Beach is fertile soil for every new thing!

As the others began to pray, some called upon the grandfathers, using Native American images that seemed strange and unnatural to me. Others prayed in more traditional language, calling upon God, Jesus, or the Holy Spirit. Some of the prayers seemed interminable. As the heat increased, so did my discomfort and my cynicism.

"What have I gotten myself into! How long is this going to go on! I am definitely not an Indian!" I thought. Finally, the shaman ordered the flap to be opened, indicating the first round was over, and asked for more rocks to be brought in.

"God forbid, the rocks should get cool!" someone muttered next to me. The flap was lowered, and the heat and sound of the sizzling steam filled the crowded, dark space.

"If you think it gets too hot in here," the shaman said, "look at that belief—and move beyond it. If you think it is too crowded in here—look at that limitation and move beyond it. Look at all your beliefs and let them go. Become one with the power in the rocks. Call upon the grandfathers!"

The sweat was dripping off my body. The heat and discomfort were beginning to break down my ego structure. My will and my defenses were being weakened, dismantled by the intensity of the ceremony.

"Look at your mind. Watch how it works. Your ego creates limitations. Let it die. Be strong, like the earth. Feel the fire; let it free you."

Time was suspended. I had no idea how long I was in the sweat lodge. My skepticism began to melt in the heat. I was going deeper into the experience, deeper into myself, into forgotten memories and a whole spectrum of senses, feelings, and emotions. It was uncomfortable. At the same time, it was powerful. I was no longer so concerned with my reactions or with the people around me. There were sighs and low groans, and someone was crying.

The sounds blurred into the background. The heat was no longer an obstacle. I gave up resisting and began to merge with the experience. The shaman shook his rattle and began chanting.

The rocks glowed dimly in the center of the lodge. My attention was drawn to them in the center of the circle. It was a place of power, of wholeness, where earth, fire, water, air had become transformed into one powerful force that was moving me into the light, into a new place of vision within myself. There was no sense of separation. Separation comes from resistance. And without resistance, there is only oneness.

Finally, the flap opened for the last time, letting in a hint of the cool night air from the outside. Never had I sensed a soothing breeze so acutely or with such heartfelt appreciation. I struggled out from the lodge and was enveloped by the night air. My body drank in its presence. I rejoiced silently in this most sacred moment. I walked to a pine tree and stretched out on the ground beneath it, gazing up through its branches at the full moon hung precipitously in the inky darkness. The earth beneath pulled toxins from my body. Mother Earth was willing to absorb all. The strong silent power of the Great Mother held me in her bosom, protecting and nurturing her child.

The words of the shaman were true: In the lodge, we return to the womb of Mother Earth to be reborn to all parts of ourselves.

To the earth that is our strength
To the water that is our life
To the air that is formless and free
To the fire that purifies and consumes.

Invoking the Power of the Four Elements

In the ancient cultures, one of the marks of a true magician was the ability to control the elements. The magician/priest or priestess was not simply an illusionist or trickster, but rather a master of subtle energies and life-force who was in control of, and not controlled by, situations, circumstances, or external events.

In the following sections, we will explore ways of getting in touch with other dimensions of our inner self that are felt or sensed, but not easily articulated. The qualities that we will be invoking are symbolized by the four elements—Earth, Water, Air, and Fire. Each element represents a differentiated power or archetypal energy that is available to us. They can be called upon to aid us in awakening, activating, and expressing qualities or dimensions of our being that have been dormant or only partly conscious.

In a previous chapter, we learned to "own" the Bitch and call her by name in order to dismiss her false power. When we dismiss a negative energy, we must replace it with something positive; otherwise the Bitch will return.

This is where our magic begins. We get to choose earth, air, fire, or water. By learning the names and the essence of these elements, we can awaken the true power within us.

Element Earth

The energy within us that is
PRACTICAL, FOCUSED, RATIONAL, GROUNDED,
LEFT-BRAIN, LINEAR, LOGICAL, CLEAR, DETAILED.

"Lord, teach me to accept the things that can't be changed, to change those things that can be changed, and the wisdom to know the difference."

In this famous prayer, St. Francis echoes the spirit of the earth element. It is not a prayer of resignation, but an invocation for clarity. The element of earth gives us the ability to see through appearances, masks, and roles to the heart or essence of what is.

The spirit of the earth resides with the grandfather of the West.

That grandfather bestows upon his children the strength to give expression or form to their true spiritual nature and purpose. In esoteric Judeo-Christian traditions, the spirit of the earth element is represented by the archangel Uriel.

A Persian Folktale

The spirit of the earth is reflected beautifully in this simple Persian folktale.

There once was a farmer. He was very poor. Then, his father died and left him several beautiful horses, stallions and mares.

When his wife went to the village after word spread about their change in fortune, the people said to her. "Oh, how lucky you are now that your husband owns several beautiful stallions."

"I don't know if I am lucky or not," said she. "All I know is that my husband now owns several beautiful horses, both stallions and mares."

That night, the horses broke through the farmer's little corral and ran off into the hills with a herd of wild horses.

"Oh, what bad luck," the people of the village said the next morning as they crowded around the empty corral. "Just as we feared, thieves have come and stolen your beautiful horses."

"I don't know if it is good luck or bad luck. All I know is the horses are gone."

A few days later, the wife awoke to find the horses back in the corral. Not only had the horses returned, but the herd had increased. A dozen wild horses had followed them home. When the people of the village heard the news, they came out to the farm to congratulate the farmer and his wife on their good fortune.

"Oh, how lucky you are," they said. "You have more horses now than you did before."

And the woman answered, "I don't know if it is lucky or not. All I know is that we now have more horses."

When it came time to break the horses, the farmer's son, who was a bold and dashing young man, chose the most magnificent and powerful of the wild stallions as his own. When he tried to break it, this stallion threw him to the ground and trampled on his leg. He was injured so severely that he was permanently crippled.

"Oh, curse your bad luck," the people said.
"My son is crippled. But who can say if it's bad luck or not,"
the woman answered as she went her way.

A short while later, the Caliph declared war on a neighboring
kingdom. All the young men in the country were conscripted for
military duty, all the men, that is, except for the farmer's son with
the crippled leg.

When all the sons and husbands had gone off to fight, the
women of the town commended her on her good fortune.

"You are very lucky," they said. "Your son doesn't have to
go to war."

And she replied, "All I know is that my son doesn't have to
go to war."

In this story, the farmer's wife looks at things as they are—
without interpretation or embellishment, without fantasizing
about fears of the future. She accepts what happens amid the
changing circumstances and vacillating opinions of others. She
remains centered. She is as solid and as grounded as the earth
she walks upon.

Like the farmer's wife, we can call upon the earth element
whenever we need to be grounded and stable.

If the earth element is missing, we won't deal directly, openly,
or honestly with issues. For example, has there ever been a time
when you walked into a room, and an friend or acquaintance
didn't speak to you? What assumptions did you make about why
that person didn't speak?

Our monkey mind (our inner chatter) gets triggered easily and
can spin off in a thousand different directions with various
interpretations of what we think it means.

Is that person mad at me?

Is she avoiding me?

What did I do wrong?

She looks upset.

The truth of the situation is that you entered the room and
someone didn't speak to you. Perhaps the reason she didn't
notice you is that she didn't have her contacts in. It can be that
simple.

Getting Grounded

Women often feel pulled in so many directions. In one period in our life, our highest priority may be taking care of a baby. At another time, what is important might be starting a business, getting an advanced degree, or getting our health in order. Which is more valuable? Which is more important? In our career-driven and result-oriented society, it is easy to believe that we are what we do, rather than who we are. Doing comes as a natural extension of being and our priorities shift as we shift internally.

In Greek mythology, Psyche addresses the issue of priorities. At a critical point in the myth, Psyche is given four very difficult tasks. One of the four tasks is to sort and separate an enormous pile of seeds. She is overwhelmed by the task and collapses in despair. An army of ants appears and does the sorting for her.

One of the tasks of every woman is to get priorities straight. She needs to learn how to sort out the many claims that are made on her time and energy and determine what is important for her. The ants, which rescued Psyche from her insoluble dilemma, represent that part of us that is orderly and structured. We need to call upon it and claim it to help us become clear, so that we can resist the demands of others. If we can still ourselves long enough to get the despairing self out of the way, that orderly part of ourselves will come forward to do the "sorting and sifting."

Keeping focused, keeping priorities straight, and being practical and grounded are qualities we need. By invoking the spirit of the earth within us, we can claim the power to keep our feet on the ground and our minds clear.

A Story of Earth: Everything Is Just Fine

Grace was a meticulous, well-groomed, fifty-year-old woman who was obsessive with her fastidiousness. With Grace, there was never a hair out of place. Everything was perfect, except that a third of her stomach had just been removed, her energy was low, her relationship with her husband was strained, and she was having a very difficult time adjusting to chemotherapy.

Grace was a cancer patient. She was recovering from surgery when she came for counseling. In the first two sessions, no real progress was made. Invariably her response was "Everything is just fine." In our third session, I experienced an unmistakable intuitive flash. Suddenly I had an impression of a woman and a name.

"Grace, who is Eve?" I asked, puzzled by the image.

Grace winced as though she had been struck. Her eyes filled with tears. She began to tell a story, awkwardly at first, of a painful secret. Eve had been the "other woman."

"I knew about her for years," Grace confessed. "She worked in my husband's company. At first I refused to believe he was having an affair. But I couldn't ignore it—the weekends out of town, the hushed phone calls, the glances between them. I never could bring myself to say anything to him about it."

Grace had kept the hard, bitter resentment inside her. She literally couldn't "stomach" the betrayal. Her anger and grief had been eating away inside her all this time. In all those many years, this was the first time she openly acknowledged her pain. Everything wasn't fine. It hadn't been for a long time. There was much healing that needed to be done. But for the first time in many years, there was a great freedom in finally accepting what is, rather than pretending what should be. The healing process could begin.

Earth gives us the ability to see clearly. It empowers us with the strength to accept the truth that sets us free. It dispels doubt, fear, depression, or emotional confusion, which can rob us of our focus.

Don't let anything take your strength away.

Call upon the earth.

Invoking The Earth: An Exercise For Gaining Clarity

A woman can become so accustomed to living for others' approval that she can lose touch with her own needs and feelings. It becomes convenient, then, to blame others for her unhappiness, still leaving her stuck in her misery.

The following process shifts the focus away from others, back to the inner woman. It can help a woman clarify what she wants and help her get a realistic view of the effects of those changes.

We begin by asking the person what it is she thinks she wants. The next question is, "If you could have it right now, would you take it?" Invariably, body language, tone of voice, facial expressions, eye contact (or lack of it), and other indicators show if the person is really clear about what they want, or if there is uncertainty that needs to be dealt with. If there is ambiguity, we work with the issues until there is more clarity.

Betty wanted to be a therapist. She had been accepted into graduate school and had recently begun her studies. When asked by the support group what she wanted, she replied without hesitation, "I want to complete my studies and begin my practice." She looked directly at the group as she spoke. She communicated determination and unswerving self-confidence. The group had no trouble agreeing unanimously that she would get what she wanted.

Terri stood up next and stated that she wanted a relationship. During the workshop, Terri had complained because there wasn't a significant male in her life. When she spoke, though, her voice was weak, her words lacked authority, and she looked off to the side. Terri was unclear. Through the process of restructuring her statement, Terri finally realized that what she really wanted was not a relationship with its conditions and restrictions, but a male friend in her life.

When she could be honest with herself, she could let go of her anger and resentment about not being in a relationship. She didn't want one in the first place. Sometimes, in order to cut through the emotional fog and confusion, we need to call upon the clear, powerful, grounding energy of the earth.

The following exercise is a simple five-step process for invoking that element.

A Five-step Process For Gaining Clarity

(This can be done with a partner, support group, or by yourself in front of a mirror. When doing it by yourself, stare in the mirror and watch your own facial reactions carefully.)

1. State what it is you think you want.

This can be anything that you feel is important or heartfelt: a goal you want to achieve, a quality you want to develop, an experience you wish to have, something you want to cause to happen, to create, or to establish (a vacation plan, career change, relationship, etc.).

2. Notice what you are communicating.

Do your body language, tone of voice, choice of words, facial expression, etc., support your communication, or does anything indicate confusion or lack of clarity or signal a mixed message? Ask your partner or group to report what they observe.

3. Repeat your declaration until everyone present agrees it is confident and clear.

4. If I had it now, would I take it?

Have your partner or someone in the group ask you that question. Be as realistic as you can about the implications of getting what you want. Is it what you *really* want? For example, if getting what you want means leaving the area where you live, or restructuring your life-style in a significant way—would you still want it? What are your priorities?

If you can't answer the question with an unqualified "yes," restructure your statement, refining it as often as you need to, until you can. For example, Terri started out stating she wanted a relationship. But she lacked confidence and authority affirming it. It was obvious she was ambivalent about what she thought she wanted. If you send out confusion, you get back confusion. It took several attempts before she came up with a statement she really supported. When Terri said, "I want a male friend," she was clear.

5. When you have come to clarity, notice how you feel and share it with those present (or write it in your journal).

You can do this process for yourself when you need to invoke the earth element. Say to yourself "I invoke the power and clarity of the earth" and visualize yourself standing firmly on the fertile soil of Mother Earth.

Element Water

The energy within us that is
INTUITIVE, FLEXIBLE, NURTURING, FEELING,
YIELDING, VULNERABLE, RECEPTIVE.

"Are you Michael?"

I held up my nameless, newborn son in my arms and balanced him on my chest and listened for a response, a confirmation.

"Are you. . .Aaron?" I asked again and waited for a stirring, a recognition, a feeling, a bond. And again, nothing. My husband and I had poured over baby books with hundreds of names. We had narrowed the list down to a dozen. Now, none seemed to fit. "Are you Scott? Brook?" I repeated this little ritual several times over the next day, each time with a different name. I knew there was a right name, the name this soul wanted, and I knew he would tell me—but I didn't know how. And on the third day, I asked:

"Well, are you John?" Suddenly a rush of energy surged from the crown of my head and swept through my body down to my toes. It was an incredible moment. "Yes, your name is John."

In the medicine wheel, the North is the direction that points to creative darkness that is the womb of winter. Winter is the season where all life grows still and quiet. It is a time of incubation. And out of that void, all life proceeds. To the grandfather of the North is entrusted the secrets and the mystery that is the source of life itself. This is the element of water.

Water is the element that gives a woman power to be still, to be receptive, reflective, and intuitive. The most feminine of the elements in its gentleness and its strength, water represents the power of nurturing, caring, feeling, and all the qualities most fully present in women.

Receptivity is not to be confused with passivity. The receptive woman who is in touch with the spirit of water senses her own value and worth. Her decisions and responses are quite conscious and come from a place of inner knowing. On the other hand, the passive woman gives her power away by not being honest about her feelings or by withholding her response to people and situations.

Perhaps the most important characteristic of water is the ability to listen and to be open. Openness is born of a desire to understand. To truly understand ourselves and others, we must listen not with the head and ears alone, but with the heart. To hear with the heart takes skill, patience, and a willingness to be vulnerable.

In the Ancient Wisdom Traditions, the water element was honored. For example, the Greek philosopher Pythagoras was one of the most brilliant philosophers of the Classical Age. In the Pythagorean School, which he established, students who were accepted for training were first taken to a statue of a veiled Muse. The statue showed the Muse with her finger raised to her lips, indicating silence. In front of this great statue, the students took a vow of silence which lasted from two to five years. This discipline forced them to develop the highly-prized gifts of receptivity and intuition.

The Light of a Holy Presence Here

Some of the most challenging experiences that I have had in learning to trust and allow the flow of the intuitive water energy have been in working with patients. Esther was a critically ill heart patient whom I had been counseling for some time. She had a delightful, spunky personality. Our sessions together had been productive. One night, long after normal visiting hours, I was driving home and felt a strong urge to stop by the hospital to see her. I was finished for the day, and I wasn't scheduled to see Esther again for another week.

When I entered the room, I knew immediately my intuition to see her was correct. The room was dark. Esther was seated on the edge of the bed, terrified. I sensed that her death was near and that she knew it.

"I had a dream last night," she said morosely. "I dreamed I was in a long, dark tunnel. It was frightening. I never felt so alone and scared in my life. I kept moving, going through the tunnel. But I never got to the end. And then I woke up, and I haven't been able to shake this feeling all day."

Esther looked up with a forlorn expression and tried to manage a weak smile; I reached out to hold her hand. The dream reflected her fear and unresolved feelings about death. The emotions were so strong that she couldn't experience the dream all the way through. There was no light for her at the end of the tunnel.

Again, I had to listen and trust my intuition.

"Esther," I said, "I think it's important that you go back into your dream and bring it to completion."

She was frightened at the suggestion, but she trusted me enough to lead her through a guided reverie as we re-experienced the dream. I held her hand, and we recited her favorite psalm together. . ."He who dwells in the secret place of the most High shall say of the Lord, you are my God. In Him do I trust. . ."as we prayed together, Esther entered the tunnel again, and this time, in the distance, she saw a golden orb or light and began moving toward it. At the end of the tunnel, she found her husband, who had died several years earlier, waiting for her.

"There is a sense of a Holy Presence here," she said, "And now he has me by the hand, and we're walking into the Light, and, and. . .it's so beautiful." She stopped and tears flooded her eyes. Suddenly, she saw her mother and father and other loved ones coming toward them out of the Light. The sense of a Holy Presence grew stronger, replacing her fears with peace.

When I left her, she was peaceful and unafraid, and there was a delicate, pure glow surrounding her. Shortly after I arrived at home that night, the phone rang. It was the hospital. Esther had passed away.

It was a very powerful experience for me. And I was thankful that I trusted what I knew. A very wise and important teacher, Edgar Cayce, once said that the more intuitively based our decisions are, the deeper and more far-reaching the results will be. Listening for inner guidance and then acting upon it is the only way to develop intuition. The more we listen to that voice, the more we will be able to hear it.

The Second Son Is Doubt

The wisdom and spiritual insight of the *I Ching*, or *Book of Changes*, has guided and nurtured the soul of China for over three thousand years. In the *I Ching*, a story is told to explain how intuition works.

In the beginning, there was Heaven and Earth. The first born of their union was a child named "Intuition." On the heels of this first son came a second, named "Doubt."

Heaven is a symbol of consciousness or soul, and Earth a symbol for the body, or the physical self. From the union, or harmony, or interplay between these two, our intuitive feelings are born. But invariably, our logical, rational minds take over and begin to question, doubt, or second-guess those inner knowings.

"Oh, that can't be right—it doesn't made any sense!"
"It's only my imagination!"
"It's just a fantasy."
"I'd better think that one through again."
These are all the voices of doubt, born on the heels of intuitive insight. During these times, the *I Ching* advises, "Go to the High Mountain." When doubt is born, return to the stillness, to receptivity. There you will find your "first born," intuition, once again.

There is a story about one of the great Chinese masters. It is said that one day, while meditating in his room, he heard a noise in the courtyard. When he looked out the window, he saw a stork and a snake fighting. Every time the snake thrust forward, the bird would yield and brush the snake aside with its wing. He observed that the struggle was like a dance, a merging of active and passive energies—or an interplay of yin and yang. The yang was the active, aggressive striking force—the assertive male energy—and the yin, yielding, receptive, passive—feminine.

The philosopher observed that the yin was stronger than the yang. For when the snake had tired itself from too many strikes, too much exertion, the stork struck, impaling the snake on its beak.

When we are confronted by anger, pain, or hostility from another, our tendency is to "strike back" with an equally assertive force, to meet yang (male) with yang (male). This seldom works and only escalates the tension.

When you are centered, you can be yin (feminine)—or water—and allow people to vent their feelings. When they are through you will know how they are feeling and be able to respond appropriately.

Development of this Water energy will occur rapidly if you have a willingness to go into parts of yourself that you have never explored; a willingness to be vulnerable, to risk feelings, to risk being you, and then to act on that inner knowing. From that deep, inner place comes a communication that speaks without words.

It is a well-known axiom that you can't help someone else beyond your own point of inner clarity. When I first started working with cancer patients, the physical and emotional pain of the dying patients was too much for me. At the end of the first day, I literally threw up when I got home. I had to "clear up" my own stuff before I could go on. Whenever we are trying to understand someone else, we must first deal with whatever emotions or reactions get triggered in us before listening can take place at a deeper level.

The first cancer patient that I helped move toward death was a woman named Maria. She was in the very advanced stages of her illness. I was with Maria almost constantly during her last few days. During that time I asked her a very direct question: "Maria, how can I help you?"

"Just love me," she said, "and pray for me."

She needed me to listen to her in a way that communicated caring. No words were necessary, just a sensitivity and a willingness to be there.

Receptivity means not having to fill space with talk and chatter. Communication isn't always verbal. In fact, it can get in the way, preventing a deeper sharing.

As I sat with Maria, I learned to get beyond my need to keep her mind (and mine) preoccupied with pleasantry. There is great power in the pause, knowing when to be silent, when to speak, when to leave someone alone, when to allow others in—and when to make time for yourself, pausing in the day to be quiet. To be still—and to know.

Invoking the Water Element: Exercise for Developing Receptivity

1. To develop the power of Water, two qualities are absolutely necessary: Respect and Openness. In every situation, with all individuals, always assume that they deserve your respect, have valid points, and need to be heard. Live in the spirit of this affirmation: I want to understand you, and I want you to understand me.

2. To develop the quality of openness, be attentive, and listen without interruption. If a person makes a statement, don't assume you understand what he means. Rephrase what you think you heard by asking:

"Are you saying. . .?" Or "This is what I think I heard you say. . .Am I correct?"

Other types of "water" questions can be:

"How do you see this working out?"

"What would you like to see happen?"

"Does that mean. . .?"

"How can I support you?"

To develop the power of Water, you need to be fluid, trust the moment, and trust where the moment leads. If you think you know everything about a person or situation, then you already have established limits on the relationship or the communication. But if you are curious and have developed a quality of openness, then you are able to drop your defenses and flow with the situation, and be open to the creative possibilities inherent in the situation.

Experience to Develop Receptivity: For Partners

Do this exercise with a good friend, someone you are comfortable with. Begin by sitting face to face. Be still for a few moments and then take turns, saying to each other, "I want to understand you and I want you to understand me."

Partner A says: "Please give me your insights on any situation that you are aware of that isn't working in my life." (Such as: How I deal with my child; Why I am confused about. . .; The problem I am having with. . .)

Partner A listens while Partner B gives her insights and feelings on where there are blocks. Partner A listens, respecting the other's observations, making no comments, excuses, apologies, nor offering explanations or rationalizations. When Partner B has finished, Partner A can now ask questions such as:

"Are you saying that. . .?"

"What else have you noticed. . .?"

"What else did you feel when you saw (or heard about) me doing that?"

"How do you think I could have done that differently?"

There should be no attempt to justify. Simply be respectful and open about your partner's point of view. Ask the type of questions that help clarify the communication and listen for as long as it takes.

Partner A thanks her partner and spends some time sharing thoughts and feelings about the input. Partner B is allowed to respond again. The process continues until it feels complete. Listening without defense is the first step in developing receptivity.

The partners reverse roles and start over.

Element Air

The energy within us that is
COMMUNICATIVE, CLEAR, LIGHT, JOYOUS,
HUMOROUS, SPONTANEOUS, CREATIVE.

At a traumatic time in my life, I called Suzzane, my seventy-year-young friend, for consolation and advice. My husband and I had just separated. I was moving out of the area, and I was in a panic. Suzzane was my "guardian angel," someone to whom I often turned in times of uncertainty and distress. Naturally, I counted on her to be sympathetic and to give me some good advice, perhaps even to invite me to New York to spend a few days together and talk.

"Suzzane," I said, struggling with waves of desperation and self-pity, "I don't know what I'm going to do or where I'm going to live." There was a brief pause on the other end of the line, and then, bubbling with her characteristic joy of life, she replied, "Oh, how exciting! I'll have to try that sometime."

Her quick comeback startled me. It wasn't what I expected. But it broke through my wall of confusion. Truly "angels" are beings that take things lightly. Instead of my crying on her shoulder, as I had imagined, we began laughing together. Her lightness, her spontaneity, took all the heaviness out of the situation and transformed it. I began to see the challenges, the possibilities of my situation with a renewed spirit and hope. My self-pity was a substitute for self-love.

Air Changes Perspectives

In the Native American tradition, the Grandfather of the East is represented by the eagle. The East is the direction of the sunrise, where light first appears. The grandfather of the East is the spirit of new beginnings, new insight. Of all winged creatures, the eagle soars highest, and thus represents heightened perception, the eye that encompasses all the possibilities. It is the spirit of the Air.

The energy and power of the Air element is the energy of communication and clarity. Air gives us the ability to see joy and opportunity in the challenge of life's experiences. And it contains an almost childlike quality of trust, wonder, excitement, expectancy and play.

Flooded by Water, Rescued By Air

Once, when I was scheduled to do a Mediation Training Workshop for the Association for Research & Enlightenment, Inc. (A.R.E.) in Virginia Beach, I had an unforgettable experience with the magical quality of the Air energy. I had flown in from Texas the day before and had one day to prepare before the scheduled workshop. Mediation is a very effective form of conflict resolution, and, in the past, I had given the Mediation Training with Russell, an attorney friend. For our workshops, we used the Thomas-Killman Conflict Mode test. We had purchased them jointly, and Russell stored the tests in his office.

When I called Russell to get the tests, I discovered from his partner, Douglas, that Russell was out of town. I told Douglas what I needed and why, and said I would come right by to pick them up. I didn't see any problem and expected a quick, uncomplicated response like "Sure, come on by." Instead I got an abrupt "I can't possibly give you those tests without Russell's permission." My stomach did a flip-flop. I suddenly felt like I had stepped on a snake!

"Oh, but you don't understand," I implored. "I am counting on those tests. Russell and I have been friends for twenty years. Those tests belong to both of us. We bought them together."

But he was unmoved. "Before I can release anything from this office, I need to have Russell's permission." The voice sounded precise and authoritarian. "As far as I am concerned, you are just like any woman off the street." I was too startled to respond.

"Do you have a problem with calling Russell?" the voice asked. Of course I did! Russell was somewhere in North Carolina on a holiday, and the chances of reaching him were slim. I was getting angry and struggling with feelings of panic and frustration. In the confusion, my Pleasing Passive stepped out of the closet.

"Do you have a number where I can reach him?" I asked weakly. Actually, I was much too "emerged" to blow up. Instead, I scribbled down the number as he recited it to me. When I called, I got to hear the phone ring and ring and ring; no one was there.

The whole situation seemed stupid, hopeless, and unnecessary! I had two options. I could call him back and plead some more—or really give him a piece of my mind! And neither one would have gotten me what I wanted.

"So, how can I turn this situation around?" I thought. The answer came quickly. "Invoke the Air. Change your perspective!" And suddenly, instead of it being a hopeless deadlock, the situation became a challenge to my creativity!

I changed my focus and looked at the situation through Douglas's eyes. Douglas is an attorney. He is a logical, systematic, orderly thinker. He is in charge of the office. It's Saturday and he's catching up on his own work and doesn't want to be bothered. Obviously my attempt to appeal to Doug's feelings wouldn't work. If I got angry, he'd just get defensive. The task then is to determine how to communicate to a left-brain lawyer in a way that he can relate to.

Obviously, Doug was very much an Earth energy, and I am Water. My normal way of relating is through feelings and emotion, his through logic and reason. I could bathe him in a flood of water energy, and Doug would simply build a dam and pull out a towel. Or we would make a lot of mud.

I needed Air to get above the impasse. After a few minutes, I called back with a new perspective.

"Douglas, I really appreciate the fact that you are being responsible with the office. I haven't been able to reach Russell yet. How would it be if I came to the office and signed an affidavit stating that I have taken the tests? That way you'll be protected."

"No, that won't be necessary," he replied cordially. From Douglas's perspective, any woman who thought that way was a reasonable person. Now I was someone he could relate to. The whole energy changed, and instead of a clash, it became a dance.

"You see, the real problem is," he said, "I don't know where the tests are—and I don't want to go look for them."

"I think I know where they are. Do you mind checking?"

"Not at all," was his response.

I described where I thought the tests were located, and Douglas went and hunted for them, unfortunately without success.

"I'm sorry," he said, "but the tests aren't there." And then Douglas volunteered a welcomed suggestion. "Why don't you keep trying to get Russell? If you can find out where the tests are, call me back, and I'll bring the tests to you when I leave today." The entire situation had been transformed through the openness of Air.

* * * *

"Nobody does anything deliberately in the interest of evil, for the sake of evil. Everyone acts in the interest of good as he understands it and everyone understands it in a different way." *(Author unknown)*

* * * *

Other Perspectives

In this age of the liberated woman, many women still get despondent because they are alone or without men. If we fail to see the challenge and possibilities in the opportunity of being alone, being on our own can be a very "heavy" experience. Or it can be a time of great opportunity.

"Honey, there're a whole lot of things worse than being single—and being able to do what you want to do," observed one woman with years of wisdom and homespun humor, to a depressed, young, single woman at a workshop in California.

The energy and power of Air is lightheartedness. No wonder that this quality of Spirit is often depicted in fairy tales as a free-spirited elf, Puckish sprite, or angel. But, most of all, having the element of Air means never losing the joyous curiosity and excitement about life. With the element of Air, we can lift ourselves from the weariness and burdens of a situation to experience the joy and lightness present in almost every moment!

Take It Off, Mama!

I was once walking down Madison Avenue in Manhattan during the rush hour when suddenly I felt a tapping on my shoulder. I turned to see a lady who I assumed had mistaken me for someone else. I smiled and kept walking. A few steps later, the lady tapped on my shoulder again, this time with greater insistence. When I turned to face her, she seemed very embarrassed and pointed with great urgency to the sidewalk. I looked down at my feet, thinking I was being warned about a manhole or a pile of dog droppings. What was it? I didn't see anything. Again, she pointed insistently toward the ground—toward my feet. The look on her face was one of alarm.

Peeping out from beneath the hem of my left trouser was an inch or two of bright blue panty hose. I had worn the slacks the day before and apparently, in my rush to get undressed, I had taken off the slacks, hose and all. And the hose had stayed tucked in the leg. Now they were inching their way down my leg and dragging under my shoe!

What could I do? I couldn't just stand there cross-legged and smile. There was no convenient place to change. And every time I took another step, a little more of the panty hose crept out from the leg.

A few years earlier I would have withered in shame and embarrassment. But I realized that wouldn't do any good. I made a decision. Since the situation couldn't be ignored, why not really get into it and enjoy it? Quite suddenly the Puckish spirit of Air possessed me. Instead of surreptitiously sneaking it off my leg, I reached down and started to pull the hose from my pants leg in an overly exaggerated flamboyant gesture. At this point a small crowd started to gather. Now the thing about panty hose is, that the more you pull, the more there is to pull. It is like taffy. It just keeps stretching and stretching. At this point, two of the most handsome men I had ever seen turned the corner and came walking past me. I smiled sheepishly as if to say, No, I don't do this often, just every now and then. Someone in the crowd hollered, "Take it off, Mama!" By now I was pulling out the last inch of panty hose, twirling it high above my head, and cracking it like a whip. I bent toward the two newcomers with an exaggerated bow and stuffed my hose back into my purse. The small crowd which had gathered around burst into applause and laughter. The two delighted men asked if I was going to disrobe any further. When I assured them I wasn't they good-naturedly invited me to have lunch which, unfortunately, I had to decline. It was great fun while it lasted. Had it occurred a year or two earlier, it would have been a mortal blow to my ego.

Yes, Angels are beings that take things lightly.

Exercise for the Element of Air

The best place to get in touch with the element of Air is in the mountains, where the air is fresh and pure. Spend time alone, walking the hills or on mountain trails. It's one of the best ways to change your perspective and to revitalize yourself.

If no hills or mountains are available, find a special place you can go to be all alone, and just notice how the breeze feels blowing through your hair or caressing your face. You can go to a physical location, or simply do it in your imagination, as a reverie. Notice how the wind can soothe your thoughts and calm your mind. We are enveloped in air. Become one with the air. Experience its joy and lightness. Allow the soft, soothing motion of the air to breathe lightness into your thoughts and freedom into your spirit.

Element of Fire

The energy within us that is
COURAGE, DETERMINATION, POWER, PASSION,
ENERGY, CONVICTION, INSPIRATION, CREATIVITY.

"Naomi, would you like to take charge of this committee?"
The conference committee chairman looked hopefully toward the handsome black woman. Naomi was a natural leader: calm, confident and experienced—someone all the others looked to and relied upon. Naomi smiled easily. "Why no, I don't believe so." She responded with such equanimity and self-assurance that, at first, it felt as if she had accepted. Did she say yes or did she say no?

Coming from Naomi, "Why no, I don't believe so" sounded like a melody. Her words carried no guilt whatsoever. No explanations, no justification, just self-confidence.

The Last To Be Claimed

The Grandfather of the South is the spirit of fire, passion, love, and vitality. It is the direction of the summer, the season of abundance, growth, and fullness. This Grandfather governs the process of life and death, birth and rebirth.

Fire is usually the last element that a woman claims. It is the power to take action, to be decisive, to make decisions. And most woman have been trained to give that power to others.

In claiming our Fire, we need to learn the creative use of two very important words, *Yes* and *No*. There is incredible magic in these words.

The "creative *no*" and the "gracious *yes*" are two sides of the same coin. We need to be able to say both with ease. Naomi is someone who says *yes* to a lot of things in life. But, like her, we can all benefit by learning to say *no* to the false demands on our time, to the relationship which is not working, and to say *yes* to ourselves, to our lives—to giving and living. Fire is released through a decision to act. Once we know in our heart what the right thing is to do, if we commit to that course of action, it seems as if the energy of life will come to our aid. Energy follows action!

Recently I had the pleasure and satisfaction of hosting a small party to celebrate a milestone in the life of my friend Janet—the obtaining of her Master's degree. It was a triumph of Fire! After many years away from school, Janet became convinced that it was important for her to complete her graduate degree. At the time, she had no idea how to finance her tuition or how she would support herself while completing the two-year program. But the time was right, and she took the first step, applied for admission, and was accepted. Then, quite unexpectedly, her parents offered financial support. In her second year, she received another unexpected gift from someone else who wanted to support her in her career choice.

One of the joys of that party was listening to Janet recount these and other little stories about how things kept working out for her—the unexpected new car, timely help from friends and family to support her in her decision and commitments.

Because she was bold enough to believe in what she wanted to do, and made a commitment to it, other things came that supported her in the decision. Had she waited for the right time and conditions to appear before making that commitment, she would still be waiting.

Many women have issues about making decisions, and they opt to remain in a state of confusion for months, even years—

perhaps a lifetime. Confusion is a condition that results from not wanting to be responsible for choices. We play it safe. We can't be certain what the results of our actions might be. So we take no action. And we remain in confusion.

Many women live waiting for lightning to strike. They seem to think, "When the bolt flashes, when the light hits—then I'll be clear. Then I'll know what to do." But life can't be lived fully waiting for something to happen. We have to make the choice to release our Fire, and then the energy follows. We must take the first step, even if we don't know exactly where the next one will take us. If we find out later that we went down the wrong road, or missed the right path, then we can always make another choice and choose to move in another direction.

"Life, you are too beautiful for us to realize!" The words of Thornton Wilder from *Our Town* always come back to remind us how much we hold back on life, resisting and hesitating because of the fear of the unknown.

There is not a better story about claiming your Fire than the one about young Michelangelo.

Because of his enormous talent, Michelangelo was selected to enter the School of the Medici. The young artist was thrilled to be studying with the great masters. Each day, Michelangelo would draw laboriously, and each day, his teachers would pick up his drawings without comment—neither criticism nor praise.

This practice continued for many months, until more than a year had passed. Other students advanced into other media— pastels, textile, paint; and a few of the most gifted began working with stone, which was Michelangelo's passion. Still, Michelangelo was permitted only to draw. And his drawings continued to be unceremoniously collected without comment by his teachers.

Finally, Michelangelo could stand it no longer. Though it was forbidden, he stole into the Medici quarry under cover of darkness, armed with his sculpting tools. His heart pounding with excitement, he selected a choice piece of marble and began sculpturing. From the lifeless stone, the curves and outlines of a magnificent stallion started to emerge.

The next day, an exhausted but exhilarated Michelangelo was confronted by his teacher on the way to class.

"Buonarroti," the stern-faced master asked, "is it true? Did

*you enter the quarry last night and defile the stone without
permission?"*

"I did," the young artist confessed.

*"Then go to the Medici immediately," the instructor ordered.
The students all knew the rules. With such a flagrant violation,
expulsion seemed inevitable.*

*The Medici was one of the most feared and powerful men of
his time. Michelangelo trembled as he walked down the long
corridor to the office, where the Medici waited for him.*

*"Michael, is it true that you entered the quarry last night
without permission of the school and defiled stone?" the impos-
ing figure behind the desk asked him.*

"Yes," Michelangelo answered, "I did."

*Without a further word, the Medici reached into his desk and
pulled out a large leather folder. It was Michelangelo's portfolio
with every drawing he had ever done at the school.*

*The Master Medici laid the drawings on the desk and looked
at them with great admiration. Then he looked up at Michelangelo and said, "We always knew you had the talent, but we didn't
know if you had the courage. Go, the quarry is yours."*

Michelangelo had genius. And he had Fire—the courage and
passion to follow his heart!

Exercise For Claiming Your Fire

Learning to make clear decisions and to stick with them is an
important key to claiming your Fire. Remember, we can never
have all the facts sufficient for making the right decision. We
can never be guaranteed that our decision will have the results
we hope for. But what we can do is make the best decision we
are capable of, based on a combination of facts and intuition. We
can weigh what we know about a situation (the facts) with the
way we feel about it (our intuition) and then make a decision,
giving equal importance to both.

Claim Your Fire

1. State a decision or course of action to a pressing situation
in your life, based upon everything you know and feel about that
situation.

On a sheet of paper write out what seems like your best option. Write it as a letter to yourself, affirming that unless you find some reason to change your mind in the next twenty-four hours, this is what you will do.

2. Wait for twenty-four hours. During that time, look for signs, symbols, any meaningful "synchronicity" that may either confirm or alter your decision. If nothing happens to change your mind, act on your decision.

Don't hold back or look back. Claim your Fire and move forward! Jump in. Energy will follow action!

Ritual For Transforming False Power to Real Power

This is an exercise for calling upon the Earth, Water, Air and Fire elements and for transforming the Bitch. It can be effective done alone, or with a group for added power. It is a ritual to consciously awaken your awareness of your ability to transform and to mark in your mind an important event. It is the moment of deciding that you do have a choice and that you are a creator of your own reality.

Step 1. Name The Bitch.

Refer to the chart at the end of Chapter One. Which of these Bitches can you identify with? You may relate to several or identify with many, but select one, preferably the one that you use most often. When you have identified the Bitch that you want to transform, write her name down on a small slip of paper and fold it in half.

Step 2. Dismiss Her False Power.

Acknowledge that you alone have created this Bitch, that you know her name, that she exists within you, and that you can accept her. Affirm that you no longer want this false power to dominate your life.

Step 3. Replace False Power With Real Power.

Be silent for a moment and acknowledge the Higher Power that is within you. Choose the element that is most needed to bring you into wholeness. Invoke the spirit of the elements to awaken that greater part of yourself. For example, if you are the

Pleasing Passive, you may need to call forth Fire and evoke the qualities of taking action, speaking out, and saying *no* to the things that don't work for you. Or, if you are a Mother Superior, you may want to call forth the element of Water and the quality of listening, or being open, receptive, and curious to others. Let your mind be inventive, creative, and resourceful in creating this experience.

Step 4. Affirm Your Power. It Is Done.

Using a candle, fireplace, hibachi, or whatever is suitable, create a ceremony to mark the dismissal of the Bitch. As you call forth the powers of transformation, hold or drop the paper with the name of your Bitch into the flame. The flame represents the power of transformation and purification. Verbally say, "I dismiss (name the Bitch), and call forth instead (name the energy and its qualities).

Example: "I dismiss the Shrieking War Goddess and call forth Water and that ability within me to be curious about others and their opinions and to listen with an open heart."

Now, know in your heart that it is done.

The ceremony does not mean that the Shrieking War goddess will never appear again in your life. But, as soon as she does, you can quickly recognize her presence and dismiss her. Then confidently choose other options—Earth, Water, Air, Fire, or one of the Goddesses that you will meet in the next chapter.

Be aware that you will be challenged by your Bitch time and time again. They don't die easily. But once you know the process for dismissing her false power, whenever you feel her arise, you can quickly go through these steps in your mind and, in time, achieve complete mastery. Ultimately you might even smile or be amused when you feel her raise her ugly head. Then, with inner confidence, gracefully and quickly, dismiss her as you choose a more appropriate and fulfilling response.

The Pantheon of Greek goddesses
reflects the diversity and complexity
within women. They provide us with
a new way of looking at ourselves from
a perspective which is thoroughly
feminine.
As women, we need
the association with these great,
powerful archetypes. As we awaken and
search for wholeness, the goddesses
return to help us in our journey.

Chapter 5
Awakening the
Goddess

Sunday was family day for our family and included a ritual that I particularly treasured. Dad and Mom and we four children would dress up in our Sunday best, get the final check and nod of approval from Mom, and then walk out the door and down the street two blocks to the red brick church on the corner.

The Baptist Church was a comforting sight to me, though it was something of an architectural nightmare. The music was always heartfelt and slightly off-key. The church suppers with good potato salad and the crusty apple pies were delicious and ample. And the warm handshakes, the open hearts, and the accepting smiles created a feeling of belonging.

I remember sitting on the stiff wooden benches during the church service, waiting for the sermon to end. I would watch the hands of the church clock turn ever so slowly, while my mother stared down at me from the choir loft with an unnerving look designed to keep my squirming and whispers to a minimum.

We would linger after the service, talking to friends, and then the family would head home for a Sunday feast of roast beef or baked hen served on a beautifully set table with white linen, fine silver, and fresh flowers. We took turns blessing the food, and then, with great admiration, we'd watch Dad roll up his sleeves, sharpen the carving knife with a flair, and skillfully slice the meat for our special meal.

Though I loved the fellowship of the Baptist Church, there was still something missing. My mother was rather ecumenical in her approach, so I had little trouble getting permission to visit other church services, which I often did after Sunday School. I was particularly fond of the Methodist service. But it didn't satisfy my curiosity, and, in due time, I visited every church in town. The only real taboo for a Baptist was Catholicism. So, naturally, I was fascinated by that, too.

I had a Catholic friend named Georgianna. One night when I was visiting, her mother called her to join the family for evening prayers. From the room upstairs, I could hear, "Hail Mary, Full of grace, The Lord is with thee. Blessed art thou among women."

I was nine years old at the time. It was one of those unforgettable moments. There was a power in those words, a deep sense of serenity and peace. A comforting presence seemed to reach out and envelop me. It was a prayer to a woman. Was God a mother, too? The Baptists and the Methodists talked only about Jesus, gentle, meek, and mild, and the powerful, strong God of the Old Testament—the God of Abraham, Isaac, and Jacob.

The next week, quite unexpectedly, I came across a discarded catechism in the lost-and-found of my aunt's movie theater. It had been there for weeks, and she was about to throw it out. Meekly, I asked if I could have it. With some hesitation, she agreed. I couldn't believe it. I had a catechism—and it had been given to me by my strict Baptist aunt. That seemed like a miracle in itself!

I quickly memorized every word of the book, including the *Hail Mary* invocation. The following Sunday, I attended Catholic mass and continued going to mass for several months, until on one sticky, sultry summer day, I passed out, overcome with the smell of incense during a *Benedictus* service. To make matters worse, the priest delegated a family whom I didn't know to drive me home. When a strange car drove up in front of my house to drop me off, naturally, my father discovered where I had been. That was it! He forbade me to continue going to the Catholic church. It was out of the question! For a nine-year-old girl to go to mass by herself was absurd, especially when her father was Protestant, and staunchly Baptist at that!

My affinity for Mary continued unabated, though it had to go underground. I no longer attended the Catholic mass, but I continued praying the *Hail Mary* whenever I sought peace and stillness.

And the concept of Mary, the Mother of God, has expanded in scope and richness through the years. As a child, I felt her presence through my *Hail Marys*. In other cultures and other times, I would have called to her with other names—Isis, Ashtar,

Sophia, Kwan Yin—and her compassionate heart would have opened to me. It is as though Mary connected me to a deep memory of another time when woman and femininity was far better understood than now.

Through Mary, I began my search for that feminine aspect of the Divine, and from that awakening has grown a deep, inner realization of the gentleness and strength that is a woman.

A Palette of Colors

As women, we have options and choices. It is rather like discovering that we have a beautiful palette of colors at our disposal. We can skillfully choose which color or combination of colors are appropriate in any given circumstance or situation. Too often, we paint our canvas of life with just a few familiar, tried-and-true colors, when there is an infinite range of shades, textures, and tones available. Why limit ourselves, when we can create a masterpiece!

In the previous chapter, you were introduced to the four elements and were given exercises to help you identify and work with the essence of these energies in your daily life. The seven goddesses of this chapter are here to help awaken, activate, and direct the other qualities or aspects of self that have been dormant. To claim the goddesses, you need only call forth their names. Being conscious of their diversity will enable you to choose from a pallet of options.

In this chapter, you will be introduced to the seven goddesses of Greek mythology. During the first *Emerging Woman Workshop* that I co-taught with Carol Ann Bush, a licensed Guided Imagery and Music (GIM) therapist, we introduced five goddesses. Later, we expanded the number of goddesses to seven. When Jean Shinoda Bolen's book, *Goddesses in Everywoman*, came out, we were quite surprised and delighted to discover that she included the same seven archetypes. Synchronicity is amazing!

I recommend you read *Goddesses in Everywoman* and use it as a reference book for understanding the goddess archetypes. It is the definitive work on the subject of goddesses. The focus of this chapter is to offer a brief sketch of each goddess and to offer experiential techniques for activating the goddess energies.

Just as the four elements describe qualities that can be best expressed through symbols, the goddess images offer us ways of getting in touch with other dimensions of the inner self that are felt or sensed, but not easily articulated. Each one represents a distinctly feminine pattern. As women, we carry one or more of those patterns, or archetypes, within us.

The word *archetype* is a term for the patterns that form the strong inner forces which are in us all. They are inherent in our very nature, even though we may not be fully conscious of them. When we look at the archetypes represented by the goddesses and see their forms as the ancients visualized them, we have a reference point to understand what is alive, what is latent, what is dormant, and what is active within our feminine power. The goddesses can be allies or obstacles, for each goddess has a negative as well as positive component. When we can "name" the goddess, we can claim the power and support she offers.

As archetypes, the goddesses expand our concept of what is feminine. As a pantheon, they contain and express all the qualities we label either "masculine" or "feminine." Instead of being limited to cultural role models for what it means to be a woman, the goddesses present us with a range of options and a myriad of examples of how to express different energies.

As you read through this pantheon of goddesses, be aware that in different stages of your life, different archetypes may be awakened and emerge. In early adolescence, for example, when all the hormones go to work, and a girl goes "boy crazy," Aphrodite may emerge. For a new mother, holding the helpless newborn child to her bosom will awaken Demeter. Later in life, when there is the empty-nest syndrome, the Athena or Artemis archetype may become activated. Margaret Mead calls it PMZ—post menstrual zest. These are the women who go back to school, take on jobs, or pursue new careers. Athena or Artemis can initiate the zenith of their lives. The Hera archetype may wonder what all the fuss is about, for she much prefers to stay by her partner's side. But for a woman who has a strong Persephone component, mid-life can be devastating. She may be desperately clinging to youth, hesitant to claim the joy of the maturing woman.

The most interesting thing about identifying with these goddesses is that, though each of us normally has one dominant
archetype, the more conscious we become, the more archetypes
we can awaken.

As you read this chapter, be aware of which of the goddess
patterns you identify with. Which do you need to invoke to
become more integrated? There is power in "naming the name"
to invoke and bring an energy forth.

As children, we remember how simple it was to become
whatever we imagined: heroine, queen, Wonder Woman,
Cinderella, Florence Nightingale, doctor, lawyer, astronaut. We
did this naturally. As adults, sometimes we have to re-learn what
was once spontaneous. The same principle applies in working
with the goddess energy. The energy can be summoned by
knowing its name.

Moving in and our of archetypes becomes part of an exquisite
natural rhythm. When our child comes into the room, the
Demeter Earth Mother is aroused. We go back to our desk and
work on our checkbook and invoke the practicality and wisdom
of Athena consciousness. The phone rings and a friend has a
problem. We bring forth Hestia, the all-wise woman, listening,
counseling. We have it all within us. As we open to the possibilities of becoming empowered by the strength of our
femininity, we realize that there is more to being a woman than
we ever may have imagined.

The Virginal Goddesses: Artemis, Athena, Hestia

The Virginal Goddesses are self-contained. They do not
necessarily have to be in partnership with a male to be complete.
Virginal in this sense doesn't necessarily mean chaste. It con-
notes being one's own person, rather than needing to belong to
another.

Artemis—Goddess of Direction

VITAL, QUICK-MOVING, UNBOUNDED, FOCUSED,
FREE, FIERCE, WISE, PSYCHIC, INDEPENDENT,
BOLD, ATHLETIC, DETERMINED

Artemis is a woman of enormous energy and vigor. She is portrayed as the goddess of the hunt, wearing a tunic and carrying a silver bow. The goddess of wild things, nature, and vitality, she rejoices in the quest and loves to live life at its edges. There is a sense of great freedom around her. Don't ever try to tell her what to do!

Today, she can be found in the young woman dressed in blue jeans and a backpack. She loves nature and is an explorer of unknown places, both within herself and without. The goddess of the moon, Artemis loves quiet and solitude and goes deeply into things. She stays naturally attuned to her inner self. Her wisdom grows from her independent nature and her aloneness. Known as the goddess of sisterhood, her primary friendships are with females. She may have a number of encounters with men, but more as adventures rather than as committed relationships.

A negative Artemis can be too cold and may tend to spurn close male relationships. Her fear is of becoming too closely connected and losing her freedom.

The Spirit of Artemis

Once a woman with a strong Artemis energy came to visit me from Holland. We were walking along on a public beach. The weather was quite chilly—about forty-five degrees—and a few strollers were bundled up and leaning against the wind. Suddenly, spontaneously, this Artemis stripped to the buff and dove into the waves. Meanwhile, I and the other onlookers watched in amazement. I shivered just looking at her. After a few minutes, she came out totally refreshed by her swim and put her clothes back on, and we continued our walk down the beach.

Another Artemis woman spent an entire college semester happily planting trees twelve hours a day, the only female in a class of men. She loved every minute of it. The Artemis woman is quite happy with calluses on her hands and a little soil on her jeans.

Athena—Goddess of Consciousness

TALL, GRACEFUL, EXPRESSIVE, BALANCED,
INNOVATIVE, PRACTICAL, WISE, SHREWD,
A VISIONARY, A LEADER, A CRAFTSWOMAN

Athena is a magnificent woman, the giver of courage and talent. Clarity of mind, wisdom, and innovative ideas are her prominent attributes. The goddess of creativity, culture, and consciousness, she loves to initiate ideas and can orchestrate things. She is a craftswoman, a weaver who understands how things fit together. She is the energy that motivates, the voice that speaks, "Come on, let's get going!" She won't let you get stuck in dark places. A visionary, Athena doesn't like to deal with petty things. Her interest is piqued by subjects of great importance. If there is a man in her life, he is usually a mentor or teacher to her. She doesn't relate to weak men. Instead, she wants someone else to match her own power. At the same time, Athena can help awaken a man's own heroic capacity.

Perhaps her greatest quality is that she can be out-front, voicing what needs to be said or expressed. She speaks for many, a spokeswoman for the collective.

A negative Athena can get too involved in her mission. She loses her softness. She can become too tough. Concern for her body and her gentleness take a back seat.

The Spirit of Athena

Athena was born "out of the head" of Zeus. She is, definitely, her father's daughter, intensely loyal to him and to the powerful men in her life. In the Roman myth, when Arachne dares to weave a tapestry which reveals the indiscretions of Zeus, Minerva (the Roman counterpart of Athena) tears it up and turns Arachne into a spider so that she will be more careful about what designs she weaves in the future. Though Zeus's indiscretions are known to everyone, Minerva is stubbornly loyal. It doesn't matter that Arachne's tapestry depicts the truth!

Bella Abzug, Indira Ghandi, and Margaret Thatcher are all Athena women, well-known in the political world. Shirley Mac-Laine, another Athena woman, became well known in an entirely different field. Shirley has a visionary view of life and has made public her beliefs and experiences with the Higher Mind, while putting her reputation and career "out on a limb." She has opened new horizons and speaks for many. She is a spokeswoman for higher consciousness in our time.

Hestia—Goddess of the Hearthfire

SERENE, INWARD, PEACEFUL, HARMONIOUS,
SERVING, WISE, CONTAINED, HEALING,
UNDERSTANDING, DEEP

In the myths, there is no image assigned to Hestia. There is a good reason for that. Hestia is felt more as a *presence*. She is the wise, intuitive old woman. Her wisdom comes from experience and inner peace. She is a woman who values simple tasks. If you find her in the kitchen baking bread, she is humming contentedly. There is a calm rhythm to her life. She finds the extraordinary in the ordinary.

Though she might marry, the Hestia woman enjoys solitude and has not the slightest concern for name, status, or fame. She creates confidence in others, she gives kindness, she is thoughtful and considerate. She needs no words to communicate her understanding of life. You can feel it just being with her. This quality can be transforming. To reach that kind of depth takes years of inner development.

Because of her inner peace, her negative traits are few. A negative Hestia may get so caught up in her solitude that she doesn't do enough for herself. She may not enter into life enough to fully experience it. If she becomes too withdrawn and isolated or content in her peace, she may not reach out at a time when she needs to.

The Spirit of Hestia

Once I had a minor acting role in an amateur theater version of *The Sound of Music*. To make certain our costumes were authentic, we asked several nuns to come and help us dress properly in our habits. The nun that helped me with my costume had incredible eyes. When she looked at me, I felt she was seeing all the way to the bottom of my toes. Her eyes were indeed the windows of the soul. Through them she communicated a feeling of love and peace, soul.

In the global sense, Mother Theresa is the embodiment of Hestia. She is deeply attuned to the depths of the feminine spirit, so in tune with it that she receives direct guidance from the Holy Mother. Once when a civil war was raging in Lebanon, she asked the authorities for permission to go in and rescue the damaged and forgotten children. The authorities told her it was impossible to go in unless there was a ceasefire and the possibility of that happening was remote. "That is fine," Mother Theresa responded. The Holy Mother Mary had told her there would be a ceasefire the next day—and there was!

The Vulnerable Goddesses: Hera, Demeter, Persephone

These goddesses are not self-contained. They need to be in a relationship to be complete.

Hera—Goddess of Loyalty

MATRIARCH, COMMITTED, STEADFAST, QUARRELSOME, POSSESSIVE, LEGALISTIC, TALENTED, RESPONSIBLE

Hera is a powerful archetype. A devoted partner to her husband and often the power behind the throne, Hera teaches us what it is to be committed to a relationship. You can count on a Hera archetype to do what she says. She's responsible and carries out her work. Many institutions, schools, churches, and hospitals would be lost without her.

Hera would never think of identifying herself as Ms. She is a Mrs. To her, it is not a sacrifice to submerge her individuality and totally identify with her husband's name and family. Her power is in a strong support role. She is a pillar of strength and dependability and can nurture creative offspring.

Negative Hera can be unyielding, rigid, quarrelsome, and legalistic. The pressure to be "Mrs. Somebody" can be fierce! Woe to the person who crosses her husband! She is totally loyal and jealous.

When life thrusts some women into a Hera role, they find it devastating. Being a support person feels like sacrifice and it can drive them to depression, drugs, or alcohol. And woe to the Hera woman who discovers her husband has been unfaithful or wants out of the marriage. Such news could be totally devastating, for her identity is so dependent on him.

The Spirit of Hera

Jean is a diplomat's wife. She developed cancer when she and her husband were at a post in Africa. She had to go to England for surgery, and her husband was not able to come to the hospital because of his schedule and responsibilities. At the time, she accepted his not being there to support her as part of his duty to other obligations. Her identity was so connected to her role as the supportive wife that she believed her personal feelings and needs didn't count. Her husband's career was all-important. Years later, when the cancer reappeared, she got in touch with her rage at being assigned a low priority in his life.

Demeter—The Earth Mother Goddess

ABUNDANCE, PROSPERITY, NURTURING, CARING, COMPASSIONATE, FEELING, GROUNDED, STRONG, DEVOTED, POSSESSIVE, PROTECTIVE

In the myths, Demeter is celebrated as the mother who would not cease grieving until she recovered her lost daughter. She goes to any length to retrieve her, even entering into the Underworld. For Demeter, life is not centered on her man, but on her children or whomever she claims as her children. Her main power is in giving birth and nourishing. In regard to her children (whether they be her own flesh and blood, or students, patients, etc.), Demeter's creativity is enormous. Her nurturing and caring is special. She knows when to hold a hand or fluff a pillow and when to step in and take action. She has a flawless intuition; her timing is perfect. She has a natural ability to love and accept children as they are, which gives them enormous self-confidence. It's the most empowering gift of all!

Demeter women are often in the helping professions, as nurses, midwives, teachers, and counselors. They understand well the cycles of life and death and can assist people as they pass through the entrance and the exit doors of life. Demeter applies her nurturing qualities in the work place, and therefore retirement is often emotionally difficult for her.

For a negative Demeter, the hardest thing is to let go of her children. "What's the matter with my son? He hasn't called today! He and his wife should come to my home for Sunday dinner." And on it goes!

The Spirit of Demeter

Once I had the privilege of visiting the St. Christopher's Hospice, outside London, England's first experiment with hospice care. The woman who have us the tour that day was a delight. She had big hips, big bosoms, and a broad, genuine smile. Her face was peaceful, her eyes and spirit serene and loving. It felt safe just being with her. When I die, I thought, how comforting it would be with someone like her.

Persephone—Goddess of the Subconscious

YOUTHFUL, OPEN, RECEPTIVE, YIELDING,
INDECISIVE, VULNERABLE, SINCERE,
UNSURE, TRUSTING, MYSTICAL, POWERFUL,
UNDERSTANDING

Persephone is the daughter of Demeter. She is the youthful maiden who can mature into the "Queen of the Underworld." First, she is her mother's child. Her closest relationship is with mom, not dad. Often the father has been absent during her growing up, or home only on occasion. Typically, a Persephone is an only child who remains an eternally youthful little girl.

There is a passive component to her personality that says, "Tell me who I should be." This is especially dominant during a Persephone woman's teenage years. During this period, she can be insecure regarding her own self-worth and have a limited view of herself. Women who continue in the Persephone pattern tend to dress like little girls for a long, long time. Often they appear youthful looking. A Persephone woman's child-like openness and vulnerability make her charming. Her innocence, acceptance, and vulnerability are attractive and empowering to men.

Another side to Persephone is her ability to go into the subconscious realms. Dreams, imagery, and reveries are second nature to her, and she uses them with great skill. As she matures, she goes through the process of confronting her shadow self. As she faces her fears, she is a guide to others, helping them move through their dark sides. She's been there, she's been through it, so she can help others. Rather than remain a little girl, Persephone then becomes the indomitable "Queen of the Underworld."

A negative Persephone gets stuck in "the little girl." She doesn't know who she is. She is unaware of her own desires and strengths and remains uncommitted to a relationship, a job, or anything. Nothing seems real to her. It's as if she is waiting for Zeus to descend. "When is my life going to begin?" is her plaintive cry. Because she is trying to find someone who will accept her, she goes in and out of relationships one after another. Persephone women may go through some pretty brutal treatment by men. They consistently attract males who devalue them. Often, they are physically abused and emotionally bullied. What do they need to learn from that? To value themselves!

The Spirit of Persephone

Once upon a time, there was a princess, and the princess was very sad. She had lost her golden ball. A hideous toad hopped up to her and said he would find her gold ball, but in exchange she must do two things for him. They must eat dinner together that night, and then she must go to bed with him.

So great was her desire to regain the golden ball that the princess unhesitatingly agreed to his terms. In a short while the toad returned with the golden ball, and that night, at dinner time, the toad returned again. They dined together, and after the meal, the toad demanded the other part of the agreement—that she go to bed with him. But the princess refused. In a fit of indignation, she grabbed the lecherous toad and threw him against the wall with all her force. The toad became a handsome prince.

The Persephone woman is insecure, and usually will submit to authority of any kind or take any kind of male who comes along and remain in dysfunctional relationships.

In the myth, the golden ball is a symbol of her true self, her wholeness, which gets lost. The toad is the ugly part of self that she must be powerful enough to say *no* to in a most definitive way. Transformation will not occur without it! When she finally says *no* to the toad, she gets the prince. The prince may literally be a new archetype of maleness that she will now attract in her life. Or it may be that because of her newfound strength and confidence, the toad in her life will now be a real prince.

Both Virginal and Vulnerable

Aphrodite—Goddess Of Magnetism And Sexuality

INSTINCTUAL, MAGNETIC, SEDUCTIVE, SENSUAL, POWERFUL, FASCINATING, JOYOUS, MANIPULATIVE, BRUTAL, CREATIVE, PASSIONATE

Aphrodite, the oldest of the goddesses, is the awakener. She gives life and renewal. She is the energy of pure sexuality. When an Aphrodite has union with a male, she can take him to great heights of rapture. Instinctive, magnetic, and sensual, she is moved by deep forces within her. Possessed of very sharp instincts, Aphrodite knows things at a gut level, and she is usually right. While some women are trying to emulate men, she wouldn't trade her femininity for the world! She loves beauty and she loves her body. An incurable romantic, she delights in being a matchmaker.

Negative Aphrodite can emasculate men, rendering them powerless. Once she has proved to herself that she can have him, the man she claims to love can be tossed aside. That's it; she's through with him. Men are very important to her, and she doesn't always care whose husband or boyfriend the object of her attention might be. The type of men who are attracted to Aphrodite are often macho bullies or beautiful and sensitive "maimed" young men who never fully grew up. Even if she has great talent, she may decide to give it up in order to marry some man not worthy of her at all. Union with a man can become a point of obsession with her and is often the dominant interest in her life.

The Spirit of Aphrodite

Once, while lecturing on the goddess archetypes, I noticed a woman in the back of the room smile with recognition as I began talking about Aphrodite. As I described her attributes, she kept nodding her head and her smile broadened. "This lady does not look at all like an Aphrodite archetype," I thought. "Maybe I am being unclear."

Later during the conference, we had the chance to go to a restaurant for lunch. I discovered how wrong I had been about her. It had seemed that physically, her body was not outstanding. She was, according to her own description, short and shapeless, not the typology for an Aphrodite. But she had a lively spirit and, most important, she loved her body. It soon became obvious that she also knew how to make men feel good about themselves. The waiters couldn't pay enough attention to her. She got second glances from men in the cloakroom and on the street. She drew smiles from strangers for no apparent reason. She had "it"—the spirit of Aphrodite!

Goddesses Mirror Feminine Nature

In our search for identity and meaning, the goddesses can become our most supernatural allies. Take time to review these goddesses. Notice which patterns and tendencies are most like yours. Which ones have the power or qualities which you need to claim your wholeness?

The following processes will help you invoke the aid of the goddesses.

Goddess Reverie

Within each of us there is a representative of the feminine spirit. This interior image is not necessarily one of the seven major archetypes, but is our own inner woman.

This experience is a way to contact her.

Start with some relaxing, meditative music playing softly in the background.

Lie down on the floor or sit with your spine erect. Take a few deep breaths. Tune in to your body. Note where your tightness is and where you are comfortable.

Focus on your face first. And then the areas behind your face. Breathe into your shoulders. Get a sense of releasing stress and tension. Notice where there is tightness in any part of your body.

Speak to those parts. Tell them to let go. Focus again on your breath. Connect with your breathing, slowly breathing in and out. Allow yourself to become warm, heavy. Continue breathing slowly and rhythmically.

Let the music carry you away from your reality. Walk across a great open plain. . .Feel the sense of motion as you walk. . .Breathe in the fresh air around you. . .Notice the clear sky overhead. . .and hear the distant sound of a lone bird. . .The breeze is blowing gently across your skin.

In the distance, a great mound rises from the horizon. . .You feel drawn to this mountain, you are attracted to it. Begin to walk the path toward the base of the mountain. At the foot of the mountain, there is a spiral, winding path. Step on the path. . .

As you climb up the path, notice the lush greenery. Breathe in the pure, fresh mountain air. Sense the exhilaration as you climb higher and higher. . .as you grow nearer and nearer to the summit. . .

Observe and walk. . .climb higher and higher. . .Now you are at the top of the mountain. Notice a cave there. Approach the entrance to the cave. . .Lower your head and enter. . .

As you enter, you are greeted by a group of maiden girls, dressed in white. Notice how they greet you as they bring you into their midst. Hear their delicate voices as they sing. . .

There is a knowing inside you that this is a time of preparation. You are being made ready to meet your own goddess.

One of the women gives you a white rose, and you are taken now to the edge of a pool of crystal clear water. . .You enter the water with the rose in your hand. The water is soothing, tepid. The water refreshes you, and you begin to swim effortlessly, gracefully. . .

Take a deep breath and dive beneath the surface. Be aware of the colors and the forms you see as you glide noiselessly beneath the water. . .

Become aware of a strong light above the surface. You are drawn toward that light. Swim toward the surface, toward the light. Now, with a surge of energy, lift your head out of the water. Take a big breath of air.

Now, you are at the edge of the pool. Be aware of the presence or form of one who stands before you. Look at the ground and see her feet.

What shape are they? Notice her shoes. Is she wearing any? These are the feet of your goddess who waits for you. Now let your eyes move slowly up her body, observing clothing, texture, form, color. Move up the mid-section to the upper chest, the arms, the neck and, finally, bring your focus to her face. Observe the features of her face. What feeling does she convey to you?

Stand together, or sit comfortably at the edge of the pool. Find a restful place to be with her. Spend time with her. (Two minutes is usually adequate.)

What is it like for you at this time to be a woman?

Your goddess has a gift for you. Receive it now, whatever it may be.

Bid her farewell. Step back into the water. . .swim with strength. You feel renewed, empowered. Feel what kind of woman you are. . .

Step out of the water and move outside the cave. . .You start to descend the winding, spiral path, feeling that new sense of having made a profound connection to your interior woman.

Find yourself now at the base of the mountain. Walk across the great open plain. . .move back now to the room and start to bring the experience back with you. . .

A Letter To My Goddess

In this exercise, simply address a letter to the goddess you wish to contact, and begin a communication with her. Ask questions, ask advice, share your thoughts and concerns, and listen for answers. This exercise is almost infallible for contacting your inner woman!

Norma came into the counseling session, bubbling with excitement. I had never seen her so joyful. She was wearing a stylish powder-blue dress with a bright pink scarf draped loosely around her neck. I could hardly believe this was Norma! A university professor, until now she had come to our sessions dressed in conservative beige and brown pants suits. What a remarkable change!

With a broad smile, she reached into her handbag, pulled out her journal, and began playfully thumbing through the pages.

"I've been writing to Aphrodite," she said. Her eyebrows

arched up. "And I've been getting answers," she declared. "I asked Aphrodite what I should wear, and she said bright colors. I asked her if she wanted to go shopping with me, and she said yes. In fact, she helped pick out this outfit!" Norma gave a bright sprinkle of a laugh that was a thorough delight. It was a pleasure to feel how much fun this was for her! She was a career-oriented woman with a background of high academic achievement. Now she was allowing herself to discover and experience a whole new dimension of her being!

She pointed to one letter after the next, describing little episodes with Aphrodite. "For the first time in my life, I am really enjoying being a woman! And I love my body." And then her eyes filled with tears as she described a letter she had written to Hestia, asking for the wisdom of the feminine spirit.

"My brother and I have resolved our differences," she said. "I couldn't have done it without the help of the goddess."

Norma was discovering a new joy in being a woman. It was being experienced in many areas of her life.

Ritual For Evoking The Goddess Energy

Step One. Name the Name

Identify a situation in your life that is not working. Write it out in your journal or describe it to a friend.

Step Two. Dismiss The False Power

Affirm that you no longer want this situation to dominate your life.

Step Three. Replace False Power With Real Power

Be still for a moment and acknowledge the Higher Power that is with you. Choose a particular goddess energy that you need to bring fresh energy and another perspective to a situation.

Visualize that particular goddess in action. What would she say? How would she act? What would her perspective be on the situation? How would she handle things?

Or, if you prefer:

In your journal, record the response that is given by the goddess.

* * * *

As this process becomes familiar, you can go through these steps quickly in your mind during a stuck situation and visualize your goddess in action.

* * * *

Ritual, symbol, and ceremony have long been a part of the spiritual journey in many traditions. Women, in particular, respond to the symbolic life. Images of feminine wholeness move us in our deepest, most sacred non-verbal place.

Be a wise woman and create your own rituals, symbols, and meaningful ceremonies as you explore the goddess power!

Perhaps the biggest misconception
we have about love is that someone,
or something else, is supposed
to give it to us.

And so we dress to get it, decorate
our homes to get it, send our children
to certain schools to get it, join clubs
we don't like because we want it,
and choose professions and careers
that promise to achieve it for us.

We allow others to determine
how, when, or even whether we
will have love.

The only way to have
all the love we need is to love
ourselves. Deciding to love
who we are is perhaps the most
important decision we ever make.

Chapter 6
Self-Love Comes First

As I looked out over the audience, giving one of my first public lectures some ten years ago, I was surprised at how easy and natural it was. Two days before, Peter had asked me, quite unexpectedly, to fill in for one of the speakers at a weekend workshop in Houston, Texas. The subject was "Dreams." The request to speak terrified me. I did everything I could to refuse. I just didn't feel ready or sufficiently prepared. I didn't have an outline; I hadn't any notes.

"Go ahead," Peter urged. "You're ready." I almost backed out. Now I was glad I hadn't. I was thoroughly enjoying the experience. My nervous tremor had disappeared, my jitters had subsided. I was feeling confident and capable, sitting in a relaxed manner on a stool, sharing dream experiences and processes to a warm and receptive audience.

The more I talked, the more relaxed I became. Midway through the presentation, Peter quietly and unobtrusively slipped in and took a seat in the back of the room.

I hadn't expected him to come! I was stunned.

All my doubts surfaced. What did I have to say about dreams compared to him! Suddenly the words which had been flowing so effortlessly turned lifeless and leaden.

What was he thinking? Was he evaluating my performance? Every bit of self-confidence left; every self-doubt I had ever known confronted me. I slumped into my seat. I felt as though I were going to throw up. Whatever possessed me to think I was an authority on dreams! (A friend later told me I had turned visibly pale and shaken! In fact, she thought I had instantaneously become extremely ill.)

Suddenly, my agony ended in a flash. I was looking at myself from above the audience. I somehow had left my body.I was suspended, somehow, looking at myself perched on the stool. But I was on the ceiling in the back of the room.

From this perspective, everything was different. The fear and confusion were gone. It was a timeless moment of total peace. How different the room and the people appeared in this reality. I was enveloped by love. I could see only love and light in everyone. From here, Peter wasn't any more significant than anyone else. We were all the same, all equal.

There was a sense of deep peace. There was no judgment, no comparison. The words that came were: *It doesn't matter whether you do well or not. You are loved anyway.*

Then, just as abruptly, I was seated back on the stool once again, looking out over the audience, without any fear whatsoever. All memory of what I had said moments before was gone. I was totally disconnected from my earlier train of thought. "If only someone would ask a question,. . .I could get right back on track. . ." Just then, a man in the front row raised his hand, almost as if he had heard my unspoken plea.

The whole experience happened in a twinkling of an eye, in a matter of moments, but its impact was profound.

In that brief, intense, vivid, out-of-body experience, my whole perspective of love changed. Up until then, I believed that love was something I had to earn by doing good deeds or by being attractive or intelligent or dependable. Love was something that came only to people who worked hard to get it, and then they had to prove that they were worthy to keep it. It seemed that love was doled out and there wasn't enough for everybody.

That moment was an experience with Grace. I didn't earn it. I didn't work for it. For some inexplicable reason, it was a gift freely given. From that moment on, I knew, without a shadow of doubt that love isn't something we have to earn. Love is something we discover and accept. And we don't have to get "out of our bodies" to find it. It is always with us. It is the heart of our being. It is all that we are. It is our true self.

Our Biggest Challenge

To receive all the love, support, and nurturing we desire, we need only make one decision. That decision may be the most important one we ever make.

The decision is to love ourself and all that we are.

Exposing the "Uglies"

One of the special joys of my life was the year I spent working with the CETA program, helping women who were trying to get off welfare. I designed and taught a series of programs. The one I enjoyed the most focused on self-esteem. Most of the women were black and uneducated. They had so little, but they had so much! Many were single parents, raising children on their own. They often didn't know where their next meal was coming from. What they had, though, was a natural joy and an acceptance of life.

As soon as they sensed that I cared for them, they opened their hearts. My fears of not being accepted because I was white, educated, and "privileged" quickly vanished. When they started bringing pictures of their children to show me, I knew I was "in." There were invitations to attend weddings, showers, graduations, and funerals. They allowed me the privilege of sharing their lives.

One day, Beatrice, a young black woman who was normally smiling and cheerful, came into my office and asked if she could sit down and talk.

"Sure Beatrice," I responded. "What's on your mind?"

She sat in the chair next to my desk and slid her legs forward. "Have you ever noticed I always wear slacks?"

I had noticed that she never wore a skirt, but hadn't thought about why. With a little reluctance, she explained.

"When I was growing up in Jamaica," she said, "I fell down and hurt my leg real bad. There weren't any doctors in my village, and the leg never did heal right." She pointed to her calf. "There's a hole here—it's my 'ugly'. It's very ugly and I'm afraid if I show my legs, the other girls will laugh at me."

I was very touched by her self-conscious dilemma. At the time I was trying to cover up "uglies" myself. My life was full of confusion. My separation was only two weeks old and I was still struggling with hurt, pain, guilt, and all the other uncertainties that come with such a major upheaval. And yet to Beatrice, I looked like the paragon of authority and effectiveness.

"Beatrice," I said, "what would you say if I said to you that I've always wanted to wear skirts and shorts, but I am afraid others will laugh at me because I have this ugly hole in my leg?"

Beatrice shrugged her shoulders. "Hell, I would say you are crazy—wear them anyway!" Suddenly her face lit up when she realized what she had said. She doubled over with one of her contagious laughs. How easy it is to accept and love other people's "uglies" and not your own!

"Beatrice, my uglies are not obvious to you." I began to share what I was dealing with and concealing. From that day on, everyone in the class would, from time to time, share their "uglies." Such honesty allowed for a deep bond of trust and heartfelt caring.

We all have our "uglies." To love ourselves, we must accept them, whatever they are. Once we accept them, we won't need them as an excuse to keep us from feeling loved.

Self-Love Makes the Difference

Rita was a woman who didn't know how to love herself. When I first met her, it was hard not to be affected by her strong negative approach to life. She was convinced that she was a victim. She was working in a large government agency in a large metropolitan area. Her boss was terrible to her and the people around her were insensitive and uncaring. Absolutely nothing was working.

She came for counseling several times. During one of the sessions, I asked her to draw a Family Portrait. This is a process similar to the Parent Picture described in the Dragon Fight chapter, except that, instead of drawing only the parents, all the family members are represented.

Rita drew two sisters exactly alike. When I asked her about them, she said she was a twin. What was startling, though, was the realization that she did not know which twin she was. She looked at the paper blankly, as though waiting for it to reveal an answer.

Rita didn't know who she was! She didn't have a separate identity! "Am I my sister, or am I me?"

Rita worked on building her self-esteem and finally began to accept her own individuality, separate and distinct from her sister. She began to love herself.

During the course of the next six months, everything began to change. The next time I saw her, there were significant differences. She had a new job, which she enjoyed. Her boss was treating her with respect, and she was beginning to develop a rapport with others in her office. At the end of the day, she is not nearly so stressed. Her only complaint is that she has to learn how to stop feeling guilty about so much goodness in her life. It is hard for her to believe that she deserves it all!

Stop Punishing Yourself

Caroline was a somber, joyless young woman. She was attractive, but purposely kept her natural beauty concealed under a dull, drab exterior. Caroline had been divorced for three years and was employed by an accounting firm for a position "nobody else wanted." Her job was dull, thankless, and non-creative. She didn't like her work, but she was the only one in the office who could do it and so she did. She had lost interest in returning to college to complete her degree and felt trapped in the job. Her belief was that life was supposed to be difficult. And it was.

As I listened to her life story, I stopped her at one point and said, "You know what I really think you are doing? Punishing yourself!"

"Oh," she gasped, and dropped her head. "You're right." And then she began to sob.

Three years earlier, Caroline had made a poor choice for a marriage partner. A few weeks before the ceremony, she realized that it was a mistake but was afraid to go back on a decision and reluctant to disappoint her family. Caroline went ahead with the marriage, and it was a disaster. He was a drug user and an abuser. Life with her husband became so unbearable that she finally decided to end the marriage. Regardless of the circumstances, she blamed herself for a failed marriage. Somehow, she should have made it work.

Her family didn't make things easy, either. Marriage was to be forever. She was the first person in her family to divorce, and she was constantly reminded of that fact.

She believed she was unworthy and was creating a life of self-punishment to atone for her choices. At some unconscious level, she wanted to expiate her guilt through suffering and punishment.

We can't be a victim unless we agree to being one. Caroline knew at some level she had made that decision.

Self-love is something we can all agree we need. But if it stays just an idea or vague wish, it has little power. Caroline decided to get specific.

Caroline started to journal ways to love herself. She began with,"I love myself, therefore. . ."

She wrote:

I love myself, therefore. . .I am going to complete my college education.

I love myself, therefore. . .I will check into scholarship possibilities.

I love myself, therefore. . .I am going to choose a career that I enjoy.

And the list continued. . .

Some years later, I received a long letter from Caroline. It was from the Caribbean. Inside the envelope was a photo of Caroline in a scarlet bikini! She had become a marine biologist and was on a research expedition. The work was fascinating, the people interesting—and she was having the time of her life.

Self-Love—The Three-Step Formula

Step One. Decide to Love Yourself

Simply thinking about yourself won't change how you feel about yourself. Self-love isn't anything that you can try to get or earn. You won't get love by wishing you could have it. And it's not a matter of being "worthy."

You simply decide you are going to love yourself. And if it takes more than ten seconds to make that decision, you've taken too long!

Step Two. I Love Myself, Therefore. . .

Deciding to love yourself will make a difference in your life. Make a list of specifics.

An Emerged Woman's List of Therefores:

I Love Myself, Therefore. . .I accept myself just as I am.

I Love Myself, Therefore. . .I wear Christian Dior under wear.

I Love Myself, Therefore. . .I release the past.

I Love Myself, Therefore. . .I can eat a hot fudge sundae and not feel guilty.

I Love Myself, Therefore. . .I can choose not to eat a hot fudge sundae.

I Love Myself, Therefore. . .I love my body.

I Love Myself, Therefore. . .I take time to be still.

I Love Myself, Therefore. . .I approve of me.

I Love Myself, Therefore. . .I take risks.

I Love Myself, Therefore. . .I don't have to wait for him to change to get on with my life.

I Love Myself, Therefore. . .I get help when I need it.

I Love Myself, Therefore. . .I claim what I want from the Universe and I expect it to respond.

I Love Myself, Therefore. . .I expect others to love me, and I am surprised when they don't.

I Love Myself, Therefore. . .I let go of managing and con trolling others.

Create Your Own Self-Love List:

I Love Myself, Therefore. . .

I Love Myself, Therefore. . .

I Love Myself, Therefore. . .

I Love Myself, Therefore. . .

I Love Myself, Therefore. . .

I Love Myself, Therefore. . .

I Love Myself, Therefore. . .

I Love Myself, Therefore. . .

I Love Myself, Therefore. . .

I Love Myself, Therefore. . .

Step Three. Always Approve of You

Avoid needless and destructive self-criticism. If you do something you feel is ineffective or that didn't work, avoid judgments and condemnation. Notice what doesn't work, and decide to do something different the next time. When you catch yourself disapproving of yourself, immediately replace the negative thoughts with approving ones.

Step Four: Self-Love Evaluation: Taking Care of You

Suppose that you were responsible for someone whom you loved and admired, and that person was coming to stay with you for a week.

If you really loved that person you would, to the best of your ability, see that her needs and wants were taken care of, that she was comfortable, and that everything would go well for her during her visit. You would do everything you could to show that you care for and value that person.

If you would do that for another, why not for yourself?

Or, as John Roger says, "Take care of yourself, and then take care of someone else."

Do it in that order.

Write out your answers to the questions below on a separate piece of paper.

How Do You Treat Yourself?

Take a few minutes and review the past week in your life. How did you treat yourself during this time? Go through the week day by day. Look for patterns, moods, self-talk. Would you recommend to a good friend that she live the way you have? Would you talk to or treat this friend the same way you treat or talk to yourself?

How Would You Treat an Honored Guest?

Take a few moments to think of some of the people you most admire and appreciate. (No limitation on who they can be—historical, political, mythological, or contemporary personalities.) Imagine that one of those people is coming to visit with you for a week. How would you welcome her? What would you do for her? What would you do to make her feel comfortable, appreciated, valued? And then compare that with the way you treat yourself!

A Meditation On Self-Love

Close your eyes and inhale slowly, filling your lungs with oxygen. Now sigh it out. Relax and empty your mind, and let your thoughts float away until you find yourself in a lush green meadow.

Look around you. The day is warm. The sky is clear. The breeze blows calmly across your skin, over your cheeks, and through your hair. Listen as the wind gently rustles the leaves. Hear the sound of a brook in the distance as it splashes and gurgles over moss-covered rocks.

Walk barefoot in the grass. Feel the coolness of the earth under your feet.

Look across the meadow. Notice the form of someone coming toward you.

Watch the figure as it approaches closer. As it starts to come near, become aware that this figure is you.

The other you stands in front of you.

For a moment you allow yourself to feel every feeling, think every thought you have ever had about yourself, all the things that you identify as you.

Look deeply into the eyes before you. Reach out and hold the hands of the form in front of you.

Be aware that there have been those times that you accused, blamed, criticized, and judged yourself.

There have been those times that you did not love yourself as much as you loved others.

Be aware that you did not always consider yourself worthy of love.

There have been times when you have not treated yourself well.

Start to reach out and enfold this other being, all the parts of yourself. Allow yourself to send all of your love and caring to this self. Decide at this moment to totally accept this you.

Acknowledge that you are all right just as you are and say to yourself:

I am forgiven.

I feel forgiven.

I am not promising that I won't make mistakes in the future.

I am not promising to be perfect and happy. I give myself permission to be imperfect and happy.

I give myself permission to enjoy being me, even when I fail.

I love (say your name).

I am who I am, and I love me.

Stand in the meadow and let all those good and warm, beautiful feelings about yourself fill you up, and give thanks for this experience. Be aware that an overshadowing Presence fills the meadow. This Presence is Love, a vast cosmic infinite sea of limitless energy that permeates everything above, below, around, and within you, extending as far as your imagination can take you.

For a few moments, allow yourself to be immersed in that Presence, fully and unconditionally.

And then, when you feel ready, open your eyes, and bring all that awareness, all that love and caring back with you.

Among the ancient Greeks
there were three names for Love:
Eros, Philos, and Agape.

Eros is a dependent-based love:
"I need you and I love you."

Philos is a security-based love:
"It's safe and I love you."

Agape is the highest form of love.
It is a love that is extended
unconditionally and given by choice:
"I see you and I love you."

Chapter 7
Three Kinds of Love

Snappy Whitside, otherwise known as Warren Webster Whitside III, took a liking to me. And I hated him for it.

It happened one day in the third grade. Snappy came in late, apologized to Miss Earl, the teacher, and headed directly to my desk. With a great flair that seemed to capture everyone's attention, he ceremoniously placed a carefully wrapped package on my desk top, smiling proudly, and backed away.

"What was that!" I fretted. It wasn't my birthday. It wasn't Valentine's Day or Christmas. And Snappy wasn't my boyfriend! Alan Hammock was! Alan was a year older and in the fourth grade. It was obvious we were in love. At least, it was obvious we were boyfriend and girlfriend. We exchanged notes and flirted with each other during Wednesday afternoon choir practice. Occasionally, Alan even held my hand. And, at least once, we had played Spin the Bottle.

I stared at the present on the desk and scowled. The audacity of Snappy Whitside giving me a present, especially in front of the whole class. Maybe it was a mistake. Maybe he didn't mean it for me at all. I wished it would go sway. It didn't. So I decided to ignore it. The first hour passed. The bell rang, and it was time for math. The package sat untouched on my desk. We were well into our lesson when Snappy raised his hand in exasperation.

"Teacher," he said, "I saved my allowance for three whole weeks to have enough money to buy Betty a present, and she hasn't even opened it."

Oh no! I couldn't believe it! It wasn't a mistake. He did really mean it for me. I could feel my cheeks burn. I wanted to squeeze myself into a ball and disappear.

Miss Earl was a rigid and precise teacher. Somehow, though, she always had a twinkle in her eye. I hoped she would stop this nonsense and silence Snappy. Instead she seemed quite delighted.

"Well, Snappy, that's very nice of you," she said. Then she smiled and looked over the whole class.

"Oh, no, she wouldn't," I groaned, sinking deeper into my seat. But she did.

"Class, let's gather round Betty's desk and see what Snappy bought her." The entire class crowded around my desk, with Miss Earl and Snappy the closest to me. I was angry, embarrassed, and humiliated. It was a horrendous feeling. I was the center of attention. There was no choice but to open the package. In order to shorten the ordeal, I unwrapped it as quickly as possible.

It was a bottle of perfume!

Some of the girls giggled, raising their hands to cover their mouths. One of the boys groaned, and another gave Snappy a teasing little push. Miss Earl thought it was probably the cutest thing she had ever seen.

While my classmates giggled and groaned, I put the bottle down and seethed.

"Betty," Miss Earl said, "why don't you say thank you to Snappy."

"Thank you," I managed to hiss through clenched teeth, barely above a whisper.

At recess, Snappy, who was very aware of my irritation, came up to me on the playground and said, "Betty, you may think that you hate me. Just remember this: the line between love and hate is very thin."

What! I was furious all over again! It wasn't possible that love and hate were almost the same. It couldn't be. I loved Alan and I hated Snappy. And those feelings weren't at all the same!

The thought stayed with me for the rest of the morning. It went back and forth in my mind. At lunch time, I raced home, still wrestling with this question. I wanted an answer. I needed to know. What is the difference between love and hate! I banged through the front door and ran into the kitchen. Mother had the table set and was waiting for me.

"Slow down," she shouted as I raced through the house. There was no more conversation until I could settle down.

It seemed like an eternity, but after a glass of milk and a bowel of soup, I asked the day's burning question.

"Mother, Snappy Whitside says that the line between love and hate is very thin. What did he mean?"

Mother looked at me from across the table.

"Betty, would you like some more chicken noodle soup?" she replied.

I guess she didn't hear me.

It has taken a long time to discover that the opposite of love isn't hate; it's indifference. It takes a certain amount of caring to even bother with hating someone. Hate is simply misdirected love. Snappy was way ahead of me.

In a sense, Snappy was my initiator. My quest to understand what love is, because of him, began that day, in the third grade. Over the years, the challenges, the opportunities, and the experiences along the way have taught me a great deal of what love is and what it is not:

We want to love.

We want to be loved.

We may not always know how to love or be loved.

So we settle for a lot less than what we could have.

Three Kinds of Love

Eros: "I need you and I love you"

• "Falling in love" • magnetism • passion • intensity • projections • fantasies • matching weaknesses • control • possessiveness • enmeshment • co-dependency • seeking approval outside self • emotional • playing out the Dragon Fight with your partner • working through "your stuff"

When we are babies in our mothers' arms, it seems that her arms belong to us, not to her. To the infant, the mother is an extension of its own body. In the womb, that is our experience, so quite naturally during the first year or two of life, we require, demand, and expect our mother to respond automatically to all our needs, just as if they were her own. She feels our fears, our discomfort, our anger, our hurt.

As the infant grows, it fights to maintain control of what it considers to be its own. It uses many forms to maintain control—tears, anger, physical strength. All of this is a determined effort to get its mother to behave as an extension of itself.

Our first relationship is one of unity with another. We know no separation, no sense of self separate from Mother. Then, as our experience grows, separation results. Very early, we realize the inevitable: "I am me, you are you, and our needs are different." Undoubtedly, our needs as individuals will, at some point, clash. And each of us, being most interested in self-preservation and in obtaining what we want, will find it necessary to work harder to fill our needs, even at the expense of other people. And then, out of a need to protect and defend ourselves, we will create an ego barrier. At this point, we will take on independence, personality, assertiveness, and even aggressiveness.

The urge to know ourselves as separate individuals continues as we grow into adolescence. At this age, we have become aware of ourselves as distinct units, separate and apart from our parents. We recognize we have rights of our own, including the right of self-expression. In most cases, the ego barrier is very well-established by this age. The "tough guy," the "Mr. Cool," and the sarcastic, upbeat, young girl you see walking down the halls of every junior high school in America are all expressions of this very precisely designed tool, created for handling interactions with others.

Ego barriers are not honest. They don't reflect our true selves. Instead, they express images that we believe will attract people to us, or will cause people to admire us and want to be like us and assure acceptance by others. We develop a set of "games" which are not genuine but which serve our purposes.

Then, Eros strikes. Eros, the "blindfolded god," shoots us with his arrow, and that arrow penetrates through all the ego barriers and protective devices that we have so carefully built.

We are smitten. We "fall in love."

It occurs dramatically, suddenly, which is why we refer to it as a fall. It is seldom, if ever, a choice. It happens to us, like falling off a cliff. In almost all of its occurrences, we are victims of the experience. Eros relationships happen at random, generally with a person of the opposite sex, usually without regard to reason or logic.

Eros relationships are intense, physically and emotionally. Eros love works through the hormones, the glands, and the organs, affecting the emotions in erratic ways. This kind of love manipulates auric fields, electricity, and magnetism, sometimes resulting in feelings, thoughts, and actions heretofore unheard of. We call this experience "love," when in fact, it has nothing to do with love in the sense of true love, or Agape.

Typically, we don't really "fall in love" with the person, but rather with who we want that person to be. Eros love tends to be very unrealistic. We project and fantasize our expectations about our partner. We project our own repressed maleness (or, in the case of a man, his femaleness) on to another, and we "love" that person because we think he has something we don't have. We believe that he holds a quality which we are unable to express, and so we want him because he has what we need. We reach the point of saying, "I need you, therefore I love you."

At some later point in time, the inevitable occurs. We begin to realize that those imagined qualities really aren't there, never were. We begin to see the partner as he really is, no longer just as we want him to be. The love potion wears off, and the experience becomes painful. It hurts to "fall out of love."

We can't accept our partner as he is, and we don't see ourselves as acceptable. We are not whole yet, so we are looking for someone else to complete us by filling in the missing pieces. In Eros relationships, we attract partners who have what we lack. And when we find the missing piece, we think it's a match!

Many people believe that falling in love is the basis for marriage, but falling in love is almost never done sensibly. Regardless of the fairy tales or the Hollywood promotions, falling in love with the right person is infinitely rarer than falling in love with the wrong person.

People fall in love because of matching vulnerabilities and insecurities, not because of matching strengths. Eros is extremely powerful. The ego barriers that we have maintained so effectively come crashing down, and we "fall in love" in spite of not wanting or intending to! We are absolutely powerless. We can't help it. We are victims of Eros! And like Psyche on the mountaintop, we are swept away, albeit briefly, to a paradise with a lover whose face we are forbidden to see. And for a time, we have the experience of what it feels like to have a crashed ego barrier between ourselves and another. Defenses are dropped while we are enamored with each other.

This kind of falling in love, the intensity of Eros, is always temporary. It is the same blissful experience that occurred in infancy with our mother, acted out all over again, and the results are the same. There comes a time when the honeymoon is over. The questions begin as we painfully start to recognize qualities in our partner that are not exactly what we thought they were. The defenses are re-erected as the two lovers gradually begin to learn again that they are two separate people with separate identities.

Sometimes, we will quickly leave the relationship that failed and find someone else to fall in love with as our remedy. We cherish the idea of falling in love and living happily ever after. We create our ego barriers one after another as we search for the "perfect" relationship. Most often, when a new relationship begins, the partners coming together have ego barriers that are still damaged from past experiences. A lot of "dirty laundry," unhappiness, misery, projection, accusation, guilt, and blame from earlier relationships is carried into the new relationship.

Even in the best of relationships, there usually comes a time when we feel attracted to someone other than our partner. It is a rare person to whom that doesn't happen! And yet, we subject ourselves to a tremendous amount of guilt when it does! We begin to criticize ourselves. If I am attracted to another, that must mean there's something wrong with my present relationship, something wrong with me, or wrong with my partner.

But it's simply not true. It means there is a match, a different type of match than the one that drew us to our partner, and that it has awakened new and different parts of ourselves. But it doesn't mean that we are powerless in the face of the attraction. Nor does it mean that we should leave one relationship to begin a new commitment.

Michael . . .

When I was working with cancer patients, I had many encounters that were both challenging and rewarding. The very nature of the illness and the preciousness of time require people to open up very quickly.

I had a special connection with Michael, an attractive musician who was courageously fighting his disease. I found him sensitive, creative, and intelligent. As his therapist and counselor, I saw a lot of Michael, and he shared much of himself with me. He was a true romantic. He sparked something in me which I had never felt in my marriage.

One day when I entered his room, there was a noticeable change in his attitude. Normally confident and open in his interactions with me, today he was nervous and on edge.

"Can I ask you a question?" he asked.

"Sure, ask me anything," I responded, not expecting anything out of the ordinary.

He paused for a moment, and then looked directly into my eyes. "I want to make love with you," he said. It startled me.

At first I felt an impulse to be annoyed, just as I had when Snappy Whitside gave me the perfume bottle. I wanted to put up a cool and distancing wall of professionalism. After all, I was his counselor. But the truth was that I was attracted to him as well. I had never voiced it, or even admitted it to myself. Whenever these feelings came up, I dismissed them. Now, I was challenged. My option was to be detached and clinical, or to be honest and just be me.

I took a deep breath to gather my strength, smiled at him, and said, "Michael, you caught me a little off guard. It's true, I feel very close to you, and you're attractive to me in every way. And I admit I have wondered what it would be like to make love with you."

It was very helpful to communicate in an honest and open way, without role or pretense. In my decision to be honest, a very real moment was created that linked our hearts.

"I'm married, as you know, and you already have a special person in your life. It would change everything if we made love."

We talked for several hours. I realized that with him, I experienced feelings that had been buried. I was trying too hard to be a responsible wife and mother. I had no time for romance or whimsy. Michael awakened and made me face the feelings that had been brought to the surface. It was a lovely and exciting way to feel. But the love I felt for him—and the feelings he had for me—didn't need to be expressed in a sexual way. We realized that by caring for each other, by sharing from our hearts, and by being open, we were making love all the time—but in a different way. We made a conscious choice to deal with our feelings. The passion was diffused by talking about it, and it didn't have to be a barrier between us.

When Eros Strikes. . .Fear Not

Every woman needs to understand that whenever an Eros attraction comes along, even if she is already in a committed relationship, it's important not to be terrified. Remember, you have a lot of choices.

One choice is to deny your feelings because it doesn't happen to fit into the box you've built for yourself. It's not what's supposed to happen when you are in a relationship! So you pretend it doesn't. When we deny these feelings altogether, they usually surface in a somewhat less direct way. Our behavior will be different around that person, and others will notice it, even if we pretend it isn't there. Or we might become disgruntled with our present partner, for no apparent reason.

Or you can choose to feel guilty about your feelings. Guilt is something we create in order to avoid making a decision. A difficulty with Eros love is that we have been programmed to think that feeling and caring deeply about a member of the opposite sex means we have to express those feelings by being physically intimate. Intimacy is such a rare feeling that when we touch it, we don't know what to do with it—except go to bed!

Anytime a relationship is expressed in a sexual way, the nature of the relationship automatically changes. That is not to say that it is better or worse, but it does change things. Sometimes we are unwilling to take responsibility for our actions and we protest that things "just happened." It is a convenient response, and it is not honest. It is important that we be clear about the consequence of our involvements and discuss openly why we want that kind of intimacy, what our expectations are, and what that kind of exchange means to us. All of this is better done before entering any involvement.

And there are always other options. You can deal with the attraction by questioning the kind of energy you are putting out and by exploring the connection between you and the other person. What part of yourself becomes alive around that person?

Make a decision to develop that part of yourself without depending on someone else to stimulate those feelings. Understand the dynamics of the attraction and investigate the possibility of just being friends. These attractions provide us with new opportunities to self-explore!

Philos: "It Is Safe and I Love You"

• Commitment to marriage • material goals• social pressures •sensible, reasonable, predictable • boredom • resignation • "what you settle for" • passive-aggressive • correct answers rather than truth • dreams of what could have been • strangers living in a strange house • quiet desperation • secure • stable home • supportive • appreciative • pseudo-intimacy •

After the initial chaos of the Eros attraction, a relationship that changes form and becomes a committed relationship can settle into a monotone and go on automatic pilot. Instead of separation, divorce, or clandestine affairs, the two partners begin to settle for a relationship that is safe, secure—and predictable. This defines their love as Philos.

Philos means that we've been through the honeymoon stage, and we have become more realistic about one another. We've "fallen out of love," and we have begun to recognize ourselves as separate individuals again. We begin to acknowledge one another's values and are committed to sharing a life together.

The Philos lover knows herself to be separate from the thing she loves. The emphasis in a Philos relationship is usually material. The focus is on the next car, the bigger house, the better job, the nicer clubs—the values associated with the American Dream. Lifestyle is important. And the lifestyle which counts is one that is considered proper and acceptable by the norm. It entails certain pressures and acceptance from family, church, society, and peers.

Philos love is the kind of love that a person has for a car, or a career, or anything in which she has an interest but with which she doesn't identify to the extent that it crashes through the ego barriers.

In an effort to maintain that lifestyle, often the deeper parts of self are suppressed or denied. The deeper feelings and thoughts are sacrificed. Issues are dealt with but at a superficial level. "Let's keep it nice, fluff the pillows, and pretend that everything's all right." Often there is underlying passive-aggressive behavior, while on the surface there is the attempt to mechanically go through the motions. Usually, there is a genuine appreciation of and respect for one another, though not a deep knowing of one another. Often, the partners exist as strangers sharing common space.

There is sometimes a feeling of resignation, resentment, and boredom in Philos relationships. You talk, but you never talk, you look at each other, but you don't see each other. You can often observe Philos at work in restaurants where a couple faces each other across a table, having little or no conversation, simply eating their meal together, passing time. A thousand thoughts may pass through the mind:

It could have been different. . .

If only he were different. . .

If only I hadn't given up my career. . .

If only we hadn't had children so soon. . .

There is the dream of "what could have been" in the back of her mind, accompanied by feelings of bitterness or blame toward her partner for not being the man she thought he was when they first married.

What is lacking in the relationship is usually not an unwillingness to change or to be open, but rather a lack of knowing how to do it. What is settled for is a lot less than what could be.

Sometimes the reasons for staying in the relationship are need-based. We need to keep the approval of family, community, church, etc. Even though the relationship may be unfulfilling, it might seem better than being alone. It may not be totally fulfilling, but it is satisfying on many levels and perhaps better than being alone.

On the other hand, a Philos relationship can be experienced differently. The commitment to stay in the relationship can come from strength. There can be a fierce determination to make the best of things, to keep the family unit together, and to provide a secure and stable home environment.

Once that commitment is made, there is no need to concentrate on what is "wrong" with the other person, but only a decision to make positive change within self. In that way, we learn to take full responsibility for our own happiness, not making our partners responsible for us. We know that our decision to stay with our partner is a choice. There is always power in choosing.

Agape: "I See You and I Love You"

• Love by choice, rather than happenstance • lowering the ego barriers gently • kindness • giving up selfish interests • openness • truth of past and present • empowering each other • common ideals • shared vision extending beyond the couple • supporting spiritual growth • understanding • complete trust • intimacy (on the aesthetic, emotional, physical, and spiritual level) • unconditional love •

Agape is not something that "happens" to us. It is choosing to love, a decision we make in response to a person, people, or a situation. It is not the phenomenon of falling in love that we find in Eros. Nor is it resignation to a situation believed to be unsatisfactory yet unchangeable, as with Philos. Agape is unconditional love, the rarest form of loving.

Agape is beautifully expressed in the Biblical story of Ruth, when she says to her widowed and homeless mother-in-law, "Whither thou goest, so shall I. Your God shall be my God."

We find it again in the love of David and Jonathan. Both men were willing to defy their king (and Jonathan's father) for the love and protection of one another. Agape echoes in the poetry of Sappho who wrote passionate verses of her friendship for the girls in her school. We see Agape between sisters who share and give of themselves to one another. It is shown in the devotion of mother for her child, and in the animal who gives up its life for its master.

It is acted out when someone gives up self-interest for the sake of the beloved. It is extending self for others.

Extending ourselves means that we are willing to do things that are not necessarily in our own personal best interest. It means caring and doing more than is required, not because we have to, but because we choose to, even when it is inconvenient. An important point to note: in Agape love the giving is not experienced as sacrifice but rather as a willing choice from the heart. That level of loving can come only when the giver knows and loves himself so is not giving to get love back.

In a relationship, Agape love is two whole people standing side by side, sharing a common ideal. The love then expands and can reach out to many.

One couple, in particular, comes to mind as an example of an Agape love relationship. For many years, the woman raised a family while her husband served as a career officer in the armed forces of his country. When he retired, she began her career as a doctor. He has since retired from the military and now helps her organize her busy teaching and traveling schedule. Both of them work as a team helping people together. Their love in not exclusive, yet their relationship is unique. The two have become one through a common ideal and purpose.

When we lift ourselves to the experience of Agape love with another person, we are able to share life in oneness. "Two become one" doesn't mean that we build a fence around ourselves to keep others out. Rather, we create a cooperative and mutually supportive venture in expressing and exploring boundless love.

Exercise For Identifying Kinds of Love

Reflect for a moment on three important relationships of any kind, past or current, that are or were important in your life. Assess the kind of love that exists in each relationship. Is it need-based, security-based, or unconditional? A combination of one or more?

Most of us are convinced
we want loving relationships with committed
partners who are kind, supportive and
understanding.
We hope for these things,
and attract partners and relationships
that give us less—even the opposite
of what we seek.

The unconscious mind contains
"hidden agendas"—unrecognized,
unintegrated, unknown parts of the self.
Until these hidden agendas are
recognized and resolved, we will stay stuck
in one or more of four kinds
of relationship patterns.

Chapter 8
Co-Dependency and Other Hidden Agendas

When I was five years old, I had an experience, one you would call transcendent. I was lying awake at night when the world as I knew it lost definition. I was transported into the future. I was filled with images and thoughts of what my life would be. These thoughts were more than fantasies of a youngster exploring what she wanted to be when she grew up. Instead, they were communications, clear directions from within.

My purpose would involve a spiritual work. The future could bring teaching and travel in many parts of the world. I was shown the faces of people I would meet many years later and places I would eventually visit. The experience was so overpowering that my heart pounded and sleep was impossible. The only way I could return to reality was to concentrate on something more understandable to my five-year-old world, a treasured line from a favorite poem or the antics at a friend's birthday party. Eventually, I lapsed into sleep.

I *knew* that someday there would be a male partner with a similar vision. There was a sense of what that relationship would be: two people standing side by side, lovingly joined in a common goal, reaching out to others.

At five, certainly I knew very little about relationships. No doubt, my concepts were limited and somewhat idealized. And yet, perhaps we all know innately what a true-love relationship is. There is a genuine desire to experience that. Yet, often what we experience in our own lives and what we observe in the relationships of others falls short of a true-love relationship.

We Get What We Want

In relationships, we receive exactly what we want, not necessarily what we ask for.

No one enters a relationship saying "I really want to be punished because I am unworthy of being truly loved" or "I'm looking for a partner who is going to belittle and ignore me because, down deep, I feel that's all I deserve." We are convinced we want loving relationships: commitment, marriage, integrity, companionship, friendship, affection, warmth, kindness, support, and understanding. We hope for these things and attract partners and relationships that give us less than, and even the opposite of, what we seek. Why?

The contradiction reflects the split between the conscious mind and the unconscious mind. The conscious mind asks for one reality. The unconscious mind has our hidden agendas, the unrecognized, unintegrated, unknown parts of the self. Until they are resolved, they determine the kinds of relationships we have, independent of what words we speak.

Once we become honest with ourselves and are willing to identify and transform those parts of self that no longer serve, then what we want and what we ask for become the same. We can consciously choose and expect loving relationships in our lives and we can have them.

Christy Got Exactly What She Wanted

Christy was a thirty-nine-year-old therapist who came for counseling. She was pretty, except that her face was clouded with sadness and etched with worry lines. Christy talked in low, halting tones about her first marriage, an unhappy union of six years. She had been too young, she explained defensively. She had hoped for more with her second marriage. But soon it became impossible, and it too dissolved. "It was soon after we were married," she sighed, "that he became someone else." Her face dropped again and she began wringing her hands.

With two failed marriages in her past, she wanted no more mistakes. She was clear about her priorities: love, commitment, marriage, and a family. She was specific about the qualities she wanted in a man: someone attentive and interesting, someone intelligent; and, in order to satisfy her maternal urges, he would preferably come with a ready-made family. "I'm getting too old to have children of my own," she explained. And so the list continued. Christy had actually written all these traits on a "shopping list." The very next day that intelligent, attentive, interesting man with a ready-made family appeared in her life.

She was shocked that what she actually wanted had appeared so quickly. The interest was mutual. In fact, almost from the beginning he began talking about marriage.

They had been dating for six months when Christy came for help. This "perfect man" had all the external requirements Christy had listed. In addition, he had just been offered a top post with the government, was financially well-fixed (in fact, he owned two homes), and was fluent in seven languages. He was extremely attentive when he was with her, which had been one of her prerequisites for a relationship. The only problem was that there were long periods when she didn't hear from him at all. At other times, he would promise to call the next day and would "forget." This mysterious side of him was troublesome.

After Christy explained the background, she got to the crux of the matter. Mr. Perfect had recently been hospitalized, and, when she visited him, he told her he wasn't sure anymore about their relationship.

"He needs time to think," she sighed, dropping her head with a sense of resignation.

"What else did he say?" I asked, sensing there was more to come.

"He said that, although he had had difficulty with his marriages, he was glad that I was the kind of woman who thought enough to send him flowers." Christy looked up, eyes brimming with tears. "I didn't know he had been married more than once! What else don't I know about him? Is this the man for me or not?" Christy got what she asked for, an interesting man, educated, intelligent. And she also got what she wanted (or was familiar with)—another unavailable man, a relationship with uncertainty, insecurity, and mystery.

The roots of her attraction to unavailable men go back to childhood. When Christy was a child, her father left home. Her memories of him are clouded. She has no real idea of who he was. He disappeared from her life, leaving her with only fantasies about who he might be. Christy still "wants" this vagueness. Though it is not comfortable, at least it is familiar. Men are still mysterious to her. They disappear with no explanation, and, as with her recent man, there are secrets about their lives which prevent intimacy and trigger her issues about abandonment.

Christy is like many other women who did not know their fathers or whose fathers were not available for them with any kind of consistency.

Though there are aspects in Christy's present relationship that are rewarding, overall it is not a supportive relationship. As long as Christy has not resolved her early childhood patterns and agrees to this kind of treatment, she will continue to draw men that will create uncertainty. Christy is emotionally co-dependent.

The Hidden Agendas: Co-Dependency in Relationships

Co-dependency is a term originally used to describe the disease affecting the wife, children, and others closely involved with an alcoholic or drug-dependent person. It became apparent in working with family systems that the caretakers of the addicted person had heavy psychological and emotional investments in the addict. They were co-dependent on the addict and had their own cluster of addictive behaviors to deal with.

Co-dependency is an elusive search for self-esteem. According to Ann Wilson Schaef, in her book *Co-dependency: Misunderstood, Mistreated*, the perfect co-dependent ". . .is someone who gets her identity completely from outside herself. With little or no self-esteem or self worth, she is isolated from her feelings and spends much of her time tying to figure out what others want so she can give it to them."

Once we understand the dynamics of co-dependency, it is easy to see how an underlying dependency on others for self-esteem can be a subtle but powerful force, not just in relationships that have a substance-abuse factor, but in any relationship that is not healthy.

In the case of Christy, she is emotionally co-dependent on anxiety, suffering, and suspense. She wouldn't put herself in this painful situation if there were not a part of her that agrees to the situation. She expects the upheaval, the excitement, the drama. The man definitely is in control while she remains addicted to the emotional turmoil.

To end her co-dependent pattern, Christy has to resolve unfinished issues with her parents, enhance self-esteem, and develop healthy boundaries in interacting with men. A beginning step would be to experience men as friends, without any expectations that the relationship develop into anything else. Cultivating male friendships would be one way to learn how to be comfortable with men. It would also give her a healthy barometer with which to measure what it feels like to be with people of the opposite sex who are supportive, open, and honest.

The Kinds of Co-Dependency in Relationships

Co-dependency is the elusive search for self-esteem.

Co-dependency is the underlying foundation of Eros love.

Co-dependency exists when either one or both partners look to the other to fulfill the needs they have not yet fulfilled within themselves.

Co-dependency exists in any of four areas: Mental, Emotional, Material, and Spiritual.

Healing from co-dependent relationships can be every bit as difficult as healing from chemical dependency. The pain of withdrawal can be just as severe.

Mental Co-dependency

Mental co-dependency is depending on others to make decisions for us or considering someone else's ability to make choices for us superior to our own.

Sometimes, mental co-dependency has a gender preference. For example, we may be co-dependent on men but not on woman. We may need a man to make our decisions, not because they are superior in a particular area, but simply because he is male.

In my marriage, I was mentally co-dependent. When I met Sean, he was several years older than I, experienced and mature. I played the Pleasing Passive role, was agreeable and compliant, and became dependent on Sean for the major decisions concerning family, lifestyle, and finances.

My hidden agenda was to avoid conflict at all costs. I had a belief that a happy marriage was one where there was no conflict and no disagreements. As a child, I did not have a model for differences being resolved easily. I was determined to avoid unresolved differences by opting not to have any differences, at least not outwardly.

It look some time to realize that I had allowed myself to become mentally co-dependent. It took even longer to understand that I had chosen to give my power away to my partner.

Emotional Co-dependency

Emotional co-dependency is expecting others to be responsible for our emotional needs. Those needs include both our emotional stability and our emotional excitement.

There is often a sexual component in emotional co-dependency. We might depend upon a compelling sexual energy to keep the excitement alive in a relationship that may not be as supportive in other areas.

Within all of us there is an innate drive to re-create the same emotional patterns we experienced with our mothers and fathers. These behaviors feel familiar. There's a certain security in their existence, even if they are negative patterns, such as anger, aggression, uncertainties, emotional highs and lows, demeaning and belittling attitudes, being kept off guard, upheaval, unsatisfied longings, emotional distancing, punishment, sarcasm, rejection, and pain. In fact, the more dysfunctional our earlier patterns were, the more insistent we are in repeating them. We will attract partners who are capable of re-creating the same dramas for us. The little girl in us is saying, "Fix me up, I am hurting."

Joan is a good example of emotional dependency. Joan's parents were too busy, their lives too complicated, to raise a child. The job of raising Joan was divided between her biological parents and her aunt and uncle. She was never quite sure her parents loved her. And she felt torn between loyalties to two families. When she married, she chose a man who was overbearing and macho, a womanizer, a man who gave little affection or emotional support.

Joan's husband was critical of her cooking, her weight, her looks, and her clothes. She felt insecure and unsure, just as she had with her parents. Her biggest fear was that he would leave her, as her parents had. He did leave her emotionally, through escapades with other women. On one occasion, he was physically abusive. Finally, in desperation, she left the marriage and immediately became infatuated with a married man, another unavailable man. It was a passionate love affair with the drama of clandestine meetings and secret phone calls. There was the anxiety of not knowing where she stood with him and whether or not the relationship would last. The anxiety, fear, and loneliness are familiar replays of early patterns. She's been accustomed to them from childhood. The drama, the upheavals, even the pain, she equates with love. She will continue drawing these difficult, impossible relationships into her life until she establishes another model of what love is and becomes clear about what she deserves and wants.

Material Co-dependency

Material co-dependency is expecting others to be responsible for our material needs.

When a woman is materially co-dependent, she believes that she cannot take care of her own material needs. As a result, she may feel trapped in a relationship with a partner or play a placating role to parents, simply for material security. Her sense of self may be dependent on maintaining a certain lifestyle. At the same time, she resents her dependency on others and underneath is annoyed at her own lack of integrity.

Harriet was born into a poor family. She described her father as an argumentative, accusing, blaming alcoholic. As a child, Harriet witnessed her father having incestuous relationships with her sisters. She both hated him for it and simultaneously craved his affection.

Harriet experienced her mother as strict and critical. No matter what Harriet did, her mother was quick to point out what had been left undone. Her mother was a strict authoritarian with unbending rules and regulations. Neither parent gave her the emotional support she needed. Her material needs were neglected as well.

Harriet doesn't want to be like her father or her mother. She strives to be their opposite. She became successful in her career, highly respected and financially secure. But like her parents, she neglects her children. Her father escaped through alcoholism; she escapes through her work. And like her mother, she's distant and emotionally non-supportive.

Two of her three children became serious problems. Unlike her parents, though, she has material means and gives money as a love substitute.

The men Harriet attracts are very much like her father. They are emotionally immature. Achievement is an issue also. Her father was an underachiever; the men in Harriet's life are on the other side of the pendulum, overachievers. Since Harriet never felt loved by her father, she is never sure that these men love her either. They may lavish presents and gifts on her, but she never gets what she really wants, the gift of real feelings. Because she hasn't experienced real love, she finds herself emotionally dependent upon a love substitute—money.

To resolve this situation, Harriet needs to open to her feminine essence: feelings, compassion, affection, nurturing, softness, vulnerability. As she opens to her gentleness, she'll automatically attract a partner who will reflect her loving capacity, not just one who simply fulfills a need for image and material gain.

Spiritual Co-dependency

Spiritual co-dependency is expecting others to inspire or enlighten us.

With spiritual co-dependency, we assume that someone else is closer to God or more spiritually aware than we are. We look to gurus, guides, "channels," and "god-women" or "god-men" to provide answers. We look to them to direct us and are more willing to listen to their spiritual truths than to follow the truth in our own hearts. This is not to devalue the role of a true teacher, or the need for a teacher during some period in our lives, but the relationship with any teacher must be scrutinized.

Colleen was born into one of America's wealthiest families. At the age of three, she was forced to make an excruciatingly difficult choice. When her parents were separating, she was asked to choose which parent she wanted to go with. To make the decision even more difficult, she was asked to choose without being told which parent her brother and sister had chosen. Colleen chose her mother, and her brother and sister went to live with their father. Years went by before Colleen ever saw the other half of her family again.

Colleen's father was a powerful businessman, but a man who lacked the ability to express feeling and affection. He was aloof and proud. Her mother was an alcoholic, self-centered, emotionally repressed, erratic, and unable to provide positive guidelines to her daughter. Though there was great wealth, Colleen experience little nurturing.

As a young woman, Colleen felt insecure and had fears about expressing herself and showing affection. She carried the burden of the divided family. Underneath she wondered if she was really worth loving. To protect herself, she became a loner who felt safer with animals than she did with people. She knew she could trust her horses and her money. They were her only security.

For Colleen, male relationships are practically nonexistent.

Two men, both spiritual teachers, have played significant roles in her life. Since she doesn't trust monied men, because of her history with her father, and she finds poor men unappealing, powerful spiritual teachers—the men who are one step beyond what money can buy—attract her. Her heroes are men with missions.

They don't require an emotional involvement on a personal level, which she's not equipped to deal with anyway. This way, she has the father figure who was not there for her earlier, and she is able to avoid interacting with a man on an intimate level.

Part of her trap with these men is her use of money. She lavishes gifts and supports their causes, partly in hopes of gaining a place of importance with them.

Colleen's main challenge is to validate herself and know that she doesn't have to use money to buy love. Her caring is enough. As she begins opening up more to her true self, she will be able to take her "god-men" off their pedestals. The power is not in them but is within her.

More Hidden Agendas

Often the Parent We Have the Real Issue With Is Different From the One We Think It Is.

Sandra was an attractive woman who continually had relationships that were either impossible or unfulfilling. Her father had been sexually abusive, and she grew up resenting him and feeling unloved. Her problems with partners, she felt, resulted from that painful childhood experience. When love did not come her way, fears would creep in and she would give in to beliefs that she was unlovable and doubts that she would ever have a supportive partner.

Although her problems certainly seemed to lie with the father, when she explored her issues more deeply, she realized that her deepest resentment was with her mother. Not once had her mother stepped in to protect her. As a result, whenever Sandra was treated unkindly, the "mother" part of her would not step in to alleviate her doubts and fears. The pattern kept repeating. As she began to recognize and understand the pattern, she stopped allowing negativity to control her. When she observed herself thinking negative thoughts, she learned to replace them with positive ones instead. She took responsibility for loving herself in a way her mother had not been able to do. As she began to express more care and kindness toward herself, other people began to treat her with the same consideration.

We Never Resolve Anything When We Move To Its Opposite. Attracting A Mate Who Is The Opposite of Our Problem Parent Does Not Resolve Our Real Issue.

If your partner reflects the same or opposite pattern as that of your problem parent, your issues with your parents have not been resolved. They are only disguised or ignored.

We still have Dragon Fight issues to resolve! Resolution comes when we allow our parents to be who they are, and complete the job of parenting for ourselves. Then our relationship patterns shift and we choose consciously, rather than react unconsciously out of childhood patterns. True choice comes only when we respond rather than react.

Leona was the child of a passive father who, without warning, was capable of going into a rage and becoming overpowering and abusive. The mother, on the other hand, denied her feelings and refused to express them. Leona married young. Her unconscious decision was "I don't want to marry somebody like Dad." And she didn't. She married a man much like her mother: non-feeling, distant, aloof. Much to her surprise, instead of remaining the passive, shy person she had always been, she became like her father, repeating his pattern of explosive anger with her husband. Meanwhile, her husband shifted into what had formerly been the role of her mother.

The marriage ended, and she began her healing process. She diffused her Shrieking War Goddess by expressing her feelings when they came up, even if it was uncomfortable. She matured in her capacity to speak out and express feelings. After several years without a significant male relationship and with many inner changes, the next relationship she attracted was much more balanced, reflecting her newly-developed identity.

Overvaluing or Undervaluing Our Mate Means We Have Not Resolved the Saint-Sinner Paradox With Our Parents.

As long as we embellish or diminish our parents, we can not see ourselves or our partners clearly. When we see our parents from a distorted perspective, we do not see them as real people. They are human with both positive and negative qualities. When a realistic view of the parents is reached, when the gold as well as the challenges they provided are appreciated, we will be able to see ourselves and our partners more clearly.

Overvaluing or undervaluing are clear indicators of our own imbalance. This imbalance will be reflected in our relationships. As a result, we will either overvalue or undervalue our partners. Either way, it makes real relationships impossible.

Jeanette's mother was strong, capable, and responsible. Her father, on the other hand, was ineffective and needy. Although he made an adequate income, he came home to bury himself in the television and expected his wife to take care of him and make all the decisions concerning the family. He didn't want to be involved. He communicated very little verbally and withheld physical expressions of tenderness or caring.

As the oldest child, Jeanette felt overburdened with responsibility. She developed beliefs that men are weak and ineffective.
They could not be counted on. Life was, in effect, hard. In time,
she married a passive-aggressive man. They clashed from the
beginning. Re-enacting the model of the mother, she became
demanding and righteous. Not knowing how to deal with her
control, her husband shut down, repeating the role of her father.
The marriage ended after five years.

Jeanette then threw herself into her work, in what she considered a safe place to express her strength. She had a series of
relationships that were not supportive. The men she attracted
were like her father. They wanted to be mothered. She nurtured
them and would then resist that role, switching into the Castrating Female and the Mother Superior.

As Jeanette began to explore her patterns, she made a conscious effort to come to balance within herself. One of the first
steps was to take her father out of the negative role. She eventually found a balance between her own gentleness and strength,
her own responsible and nurturing sides. The result was that she
attracted a more integrated partner.

Anna's mother lived for her husband in a self-sacrificing
manner. She lacked a good sense of her own identity and tended
to be non-communicative and passive-aggressive. Anna's father
was a highly successful professional man with wide interests and
sophisticated tastes, a lover of the arts, music, and culture. He
offered Anna positive values and clear guidance, though he was
controlling and rigid at times.

For Anna, the parent on the pedestal was her father. She, like
him, became a high achiever and chose a profession he encouraged. Even in appearance, she attempted to be male-like.
Since she values men more than women, her friendships are
almost exclusively with men. Her significant-other relationship
is a carbon copy of her father. He is an older, refined, successful,
professional man, who is strongly opinionated, dominating, and
inflexible.

Although Anna is highly successful as an attorney, she is still
looking for guidance and approval from a strong male. She views
her mother as weak and ineffective and unconsciously wants to
be the opposite of her, although she repeats her pattern of
dependence on the dominant male. Anna undervalues the female

part of herself: the emotions, the feelings, the ability to nurture. When Anna opens to this part of herself, acknowledging that gentleness can be strength as well, she will no longer re-create her childhood pattern. Also, she will enjoy female friends.

Every Person That We Attract In Our Life
Mirrors Some Part of Ourselves, Even If
It Is Not Obvious What That Match Is.

When someone does something that triggers us, it is because that person, in some way, mirrors us. He or she reflects either a replica or a exaggeration of a quality we possess and have not yet integrated. In other words, what we react to most in other people is that part of ourselves that we haven't owned or acknowledged. The mirror is there, even if it is not obvious. For example, when writing this book, I was assisted by a friend who is both sensitive and a creative writer. One day he called to say that he had lost a couple of pages from the manuscript. What! "Lost" a couple of pages. How could he? This astounded me. It was mind-boggling! Now I would have to re-create those pages. I went back to my computer, muttering, "How in the world could he lose a couple of pages?" The funny thing was I couldn't find the pages that I had just been working on! He was a perfect mirror! Instead of judging him for being scattered, I could see in him that part in me that needs to be better organized. At the same time, his creativity and mine mirror also.

Exercise For Looking At Co-dependency

Take another look at the same three relationships you used for the previous exercise. Consider whether these relationships reflect one or more of the four kinds of co-dependencies. Do you recognize the same patterns of co-dependent behavior in all three relationships, or are your co-dependent patterns different in each relationship?

The purpose of all relationships
is to become conscious and to awaken love.

Being conscious means taking
responsibility for both the kinds of
partners we attract and the quality of those
relationships.

Chapter 9
Partners We Attract
and Why

"Who should I be today?" I would ask my older brother, John, as we played our favorite game. "Should I be Betty or David?" And John would decide my identity for the game.

It never occurred to me that I could make the choice for myself. John was my best friend, my constant companion.

We were a close brother-and-sister team, growing up in the Ozzie and Harriet era of the '50s in Front Royal, Virginia, a small, picturesque town nestled at the foothills of the Blue Ridge Mountains. It was an era when women, for the most part, played the traditional role of wife and mother, and when men, for the most part, were the heads of families and made all the important decisions.

My idea of what it was to be a female was confined to the limited cultural models of the '50s and Small Town, USA. It is not surprising that I depended upon John, the significant male in my life, to give me the permission I needed to express the freer part of my nature. I was afraid of claiming my own power and making my own decisions.

If John said "Be Betty," I would let my long, blonde hair flow freely, put on a pretty dress and shiny black patent leather shoes. We played store, school, or church, or I would dutifully clean up my room and practice the piano. Betty was supposed to be pretty, pleasing, and agreeable. At times, I felt victimized, betrayed, and angry that the adventuresome, fun-loving, outgoing me was being squelched.

On the days when John said "Be David, " I would get a glint in my eye, run into my room, braid my hair, put on jeans and sneakers, and off we'd go, running, climbing, laughing and rough-housing, exploring jungles, fighting battles, and creating adventure. It was exciting to be David. He was bold, assertive, and competitive. And David, on the other hand, could be overly demanding, making me feel scared, alone, and abandoned.

For years I continued to require men to tell me who I could be at any given moment, be it Betty or David. I became what my boyfriends, husband, bosses, and teachers expected of me. I had no idea that there was another option. It took many years before I realized that it wasn't a matter of being either "David" or "Betty." I could merge both parts of myself, both female and male, and become a whole woman. I could be both gentle and strong.

Purpose of Relationships

The purpose of all relationships is to become conscious and to awaken love. Being conscious means taking responsibility for the partners we attract and the quality of our relationships.

Being conscious also means that when we notice that what we are doing is not serving us, or when we realize we are regressing back into old patterns, we change. And we change quickly, not waiting sixty years, or six years, or six months, but noticing and shifting within six minutes or even six seconds. We create our patterns, and we can transform them. We can be who we want to be.

The real nature of woman is love. We want to both express love and receive love graciously. All relationships are opportunities to practice and learn about love.

Usually, the term *relationship* or *partnership* implies the significant other in our lives. I am defining *partnership* or *relationship* to include not just significant others but all those who are in our inner circle. These partners would include children, bosses, teachers, friends, business partners, etc.

To a lesser degree, relationships and partners would include those in our outer circle: everyone from the neighbor down the street, to whom we talk occasionally, to the sales clerk with whom we have only brief interactions, to nodding passersby on the street. In the broadest sense, the outer circle would include everyone on the planet. Just by the fact that we share space together on the earth means we impact each other. We are committed to destroying or enhancing life for one another.

Some of us have chosen one committed relationship, and our lessons are usually mirrored through that person. Others have had a series of relationships, with lessons that accompany each relationship. And still others are not in any significant-other relationship. There are many reasons for that: we are scared, we are in the process of healing, we have chosen not to be for a variety of reasons, real and unreal, or we don't know why.

We can't avoid learning; if we are in a committed relationship, most of our learning about love will probably be in that partnership. If we are not in a committed partnership, it means that life will present our lessons in other ways. Even our waitress at a restaurant, whose name we do not know, is quite capable of being our perfect mirror.

No matter what life situations we have chosen for ourselves, we will interact with many relationships, many partners of various kinds in our lives.

Our choice is not whether we have partnerships. That is a given. The choice is only with whom we want to learn and whether we want to avoid, deny, or prolong the time that it takes for us to learn.

The most important relationship we will ever have is the one with self. All other relationships are an extension of that one. The kinds of relationships we have, therefore, are totally up to us. The only person who ever has to change to make a relationship different is ourselves. As we change, those around us automatically reflect that change. We teach people how to treat us. According to their response, we will know what we believe about ourselves.

It is imperative for any woman who is interested in transformation to examine honestly the partnerships that she has attracted, particularly those in her inner circle:

Be willing to look at:

• The positive qualities that attracted you to this person (this person mirrors your qualities, ones you may be aware of or those you are beginning to develop)

• The negative qualities (your disowned parts)

• The response to this person that didn't work (for example: The Shrieking War Goddess)

• Co-dependency patterns (emotional, mental, physical or spiritual co-dependency)

• The gold: what was the value from the relationship? What did you learn—the positive change?

My Personal Purpose

From earliest childhood, I had carried a strong inner knowledge that my purpose in life was to do a spiritual work. This feeling of a "calling" began at about the age of four and stayed until my last years in college. I can't remember a time when I wasn't intrigued with things of the spirit, the mysteries of the inner life. The part of me that was called to do a spiritual work I called "Elizabeth." And there was "Mary"—the part of me that was intrigued with the mystical, the inner world of dreams and intuition. These were hidden parts of myself which few people knew. Almost everybody called me "Betty."

In college, I wrote away to several seminaries. I thought both my work and my purpose in life could be fulfilled by a life in the ministry. But the responses were disappointing. The programs seemed too confined, too rigid, limiting and constricting. There seemed no place to explore what I was looking for, no place where I could study the things that fascinated me the most. Near the end of my college years, I began to lose my faith in the dream. I began to listen to "Betty," that side of myself that had been taught by many voices that "Life isn't like that. Be reasonable, get practical. Get your head out of the clouds. Stop being a dreamer!"

No special partner appeared with a shared vision. And then I met Sean, the man who became my husband. Sean didn't know about the "Mary" me or about "Elizabeth." He married "Betty," and Sean and Betty had everything that society considers the ideal—the perfect marriage. Sean was the prominent attorney. Betty was his attractive, competent, educated wife. We had a big home on the river, lots of status and plenty of money. We had everything except a common goal and a shared ideal. A relationship without those will always be a limited one. For seventeen years, I concerned myself with form, appearance, and role, constantly trying to live up to what others expected me to be. Betty opted for comfort and security and in exchange surrendered her connection to that deeply-felt sense of spirit and to that intuitive knowing that her life was to be one of service. In Betty's life there was little room for Mary, and no work for Elizabeth. They withdrew into some forgotten place inside me, and I lost their address.

Eventually my marriage came to an end. At the time, I thought it was because Sean and I did not share the same ideal, and I wanted to grow. There was no room to breathe, and an underlying restlessness that was not being dealt with. I didn't know then that it was possible to make changes within myself and within the marriage. It seemed divorce was the only option.

Positive Qualities	Challenging Qualities	Response

Similar background
Responsible
Family man
Financial security
Warm
Secure
	Philosophical
	  differences
	Suppressed
	  feelings
	Control
		Pleasing
		Passive

Co-Dependency	Gold

Mental
(Making major
  family decisions
  and choices about
  life-style)
Material (financial
  security)
	*Motherhood
	*Find own identity
	  and change the
	  direction of
	  my life
	*Stability

With the divorce came that painful, awesome, confusing, challenging experience of being a woman in transition. A woman in transition is almost always unclear and uncertain. She is no longer the person she used to be—and she doesn't know yet who she is. If the relationship ends because the man leaves her, she is angry. If she ends the relationship, she feels guilty.

Women In Transition

When a woman is in transition, she struggles with the beliefs, patterns, and expectations of the past and with a diffuse and unformed future. She is likely to swing from one extreme to another—from being prim and proper perhaps, to being reckless and adventurous. She often makes rash, impulsive choices with painful results. At the same time, the transitional phase can be a period of risk-taking, fun, and experimentation. It can also be a rich period, of deep inner reflection and self-discovery. My transition was all of those things.

Relationships which begin during a time of transition seldom last. When a woman is in transition, she attracts men who mirror her sense of incompleteness. The relationships tend to be one of three distinct categories. They can be "fast burners," "repeat performances," or "swing" relationships.

The "fast burners" are intense, with a lot of fire, but short-lived. In these relationships, we access and release emotions formerly denied. The "repeat performance" is a duplicate of what was just left. It's the old stuff all over again, only with new names and new places. Once we see the correlation of the old relationship with the present one, we may want to make a quick exit or make the determination to somehow make it different this time. The most difficult dilemma is that we don't see the similarity between the two relationships. In the "swing" relationship you attract the exact opposite of the relationship you just left. It is a swing to the other side of the pendulum, which means you're still dealing with the same issue.

Whatever the experience we are drawn to, we are de-mystifying our illusions and learning about real love. Our partners can be our greatest teachers because they force us to see ourselves.

During my transitional period, three male figures became significant, each mirroring different aspects of myself. Two of the men were already friends; but with the change in my life, they took on different roles.

It is not surprising that after my safe, secure, and predictable marriage dissolved into divorce, the next phase of my life would be a startling contrast to everything I had known before. At some level, I knew I needed a crash course in opening up—and that's what I attracted.

Opening The Heart—Jason

Jason was delightful, charming, fun-loving, generous, im-aginative, wise, creative, and, above all, magical. Jason was constantly celebrating the simple joy and the great blessing of being alive in a universe filled with the most incredible and delightful surprises, like seashells and fairy tales, rainbows and music. With Jason, time always seemed suspended. I might not see him for months, and then we would spend a couple of days together and it would seem that months or years of adventure, excitement, magic, and incredible peace were compressed into those brief hours. He indeed was a mystic, a man with a rich and deep inner nature. With Jason, I learned the language of dreams, the world of symbols and subtle energies. It was through him that dreams became my best friends. I looked to them for guidance, accepted their wisdom, and trusted them completely. He had a profound understanding of the dream world, and I had an aptitude and an eagerness to learn. Also Jason encouraged me to develop inner disciplines: to practice yoga, to appreciate solitude, and to listen from within. To Jason, people were sounds and scents, and I began to see and hear with his sensitivity. Above all else, Jason had an open heart. His greatest gift to me was his ability to make me feel loved, valued, and appreciated as a woman.

The relationship encompassed a nine-year period. We were dear friends, sometimes brother and sister, or sometimes teacher and student, and eventually lovers. In many ways we were cut out of the same cloth. There was always a special grace surround-ing our union, as though there was some kind of divine dispen-sation. Often, magical things seemed to happen when we were together. I began to understand the phenomenon of "synchronicity." If we decided we wanted some apple pie, at the next corner there would be a sign saying "Today's Special— Apple Pie"! If we ventured into the woods, a mist would sud-denly appear, making the setting more charmed. I would be teaching in California and circumstances would bring Jason to the same place at the same time. The pieces on the giant chess board definitely moved in our favor.

Jason was quick to help me with difficult decisions and ready to help me see another perspective. He was the knight who did battle for me. (Later I recognized aspects of mental and spiritual co-dependency.) If I ever needed him, I would simply think of him and within twenty-four hours there would be a welcome "Mary, what's on your mind?" Somehow it seemed our relationship was not limited by time or space. At some other level we were deeply, perhaps eternally, connected.

Then it began to unravel. Seeing each other only periodically over the years limited our relationship. How lofty and lovely things can be when meetings are only intermittent and in unfamiliar and exotic settings. But when it is time to spend extended time together, the inevitable occurs.

We had gone away to the Outer Banks of North Carolina to design some workshops together. As long as we focused on our work, things went well and the creativity kept flowing. But when things switched to the personal level, I felt a dominance and over-control from Jason. From his perspective, he was simply trying to help me get through some "stuff." By now, I was weary of his teacher role. It wasn't what I wanted or needed. Jason dominated too much of the time. Jason was the teacher and I was the favorite student. However, no games can be continued unless, at some level, both agree to keep playing.

Every relationship requires graceful shifts in roles; sometimes we might be brother-sister, mother-child, father-daughter, or teacher-student to one another. But if we get over-identified in one role, it makes a real friendship and partnership impossible. There was another issue, though, that went much deeper and that I couldn't see until much later. I was still in La-La Land, not wanting to risk and commit totally to any one thing or any one partner. Jason had been patient and infinitely resourceful in presenting relationship possibilities, but the time for patience was over. He was definitely a knight on a quest, but his quest would take him in a different direction.

The return trip was bittersweet, an ominous prelude for the inevitable finale. Whereas we had always sensed a sphere of love and protection surrounding us, it had somehow vanished, leaving a noticeable vacuum. Everything was off. To begin with, when we left the hotel, we missed the ferry. While we waited for the next one, we took a walk on a desolate beach strewn with dead fish. On the road back to Virginia Beach, a German Shepherd leapt out from the bushes. Jason swerved to avoid the dog, but not in time. The Shepherd was stunned and ran off limping and whining into the woods. We searched for her and even went to the local store to try to identify the owner, but to no avail. What made this episode so potent was that twice before a German Shepherd had saved Jason's life. It was clear. The magic had left us. We were not able to move the relationship to the next level. After nine years, the relationship had run its course. It was over and it was painful.

Several years later, I had a lucid dream. In my dream, a friend from Holland was telling me her dream. As she recounted the dream, I began interpreting it for her. The interpretation flowed clearly and effortlessly, as if Jason were speaking through me. It was exactly the kind of clarity I had seen him demonstrate many times. Now I was experiencing it myself.

At our last meeting, Jason had said I no longer needed him. I could see it was true. Through his sensitivity and depth, he had given me a powerful gift. With this dream, I knew how powerful that gift was. The transfer was complete. Some relationships are not forever. They are given for a particular time and a special purpose. He had been my guide, my bridge from one world to another. But there comes a time when you must walk on your own. I no longer needed Jason to reflect the Mary that was awake.

Positive Qualities	Challenging Qualities	Response
Creative Sensitive Generous Intuitive Optimistic Supportive Open hearted Wise	Secrecy Higher/lower games Loner	Pleasing Passive

Co-Dependency	Gold

Mental (clarity)
Spiritual (wisdom)
	*Love and
	    appreciate life
	*Heightened
	    sensitivity
	*Value self
	    as a woman
	*Depth/intuition

No Turning Back—Peter

The urgency in my brother's voice first prodded me to meet Peter. James and I had spent several years together studying and discussing the Source material channeled by the great American clairvoyant, Edgar Cayce. James was convinced that Peter Davidson was as gifted a psychic as Cayce.

At that time, I was sure my "guru" stage was over. I had already made a pilgrimage to India to explore the wisdom of the East. There I met a spiritual teacher and we began a correspondence that lasted for two years. I felt I had outgrown the need for that relationship and wasn't looking for another outer teacher to guide my inner growth. So it was with some reluctance that I agreed to meet James in Virginia Beach at the center where Peter conducted his Sunday service. I had just parked the car several blocks from the center and was pulling the keys out of the ignition, when I noticed a man walking down the street.

His physical appearance in no way attracted me; yet there was something magnetic and very familiar about him. His salt-and-pepper hair was slicked back in a way I found unappealing. He was dressed in a frumpy brown polyester suit and wore a matching gold tie and shirt. And polyester was something I had a strong prejudice against. Not only that, but it was a tasteless combination of colors, from my judgmental perspective. My rational mind could come up with reasons to dismiss him. And yet, my feeling self found him most appealing.

What was this uncanny familiarity I felt with this stranger? From where and from when? I flashed back to my childhood *deja vu*. I suddenly recalled his face from a sea of many I had seen on the screen during that flash into the future I had experienced as a child. I somehow knew him already. There was a vitality about this stranger, a certain enthusiasm as he walked, a sense that he walked with God. "That must be Peter," I thought. Even at a distance I felt power radiating from him and sensed an inner connection. A power surged through my body like an electrical current, from the crown of my head to the tip of my toes. I sat in the car for some time, wondering if I should go into that service. If I did, I somehow knew my life would never be the same. My premonition proved correct.

Peter conducted a communion service that day. The blessing

he gave was "Expect to be changed by this experience." And I was! There was no turning back. Elizabeth, the woman with a purpose, had been awakened.

There was something so alive in Peter's words, so clear in his teachings, that a slumbering, dormant part of me responded immediately to his words. And I felt a spiritual depth, a return to my real self. My association with Peter lasted twelve years. During that time, he was a mentor, beloved friend, and brother— and the most outrageous, paradoxical, and unpredictable human I have ever known.

Almost from the start, Peter encouraged me to teach. Often, I taught with him in a variety of settings: London, New York, California, Texas, Israel. Other times, I was off teaching by myself. Being with him sparked my creativity and challenged my mind and capacities to the utmost. I loved being pushed to the edge.

One of my first experiences with Peter remains one of my most treasured. My brother James and I were visiting Peter, chatting in his living room, when there was a loud insistent banging at the door. In bounded a disheveled man of about forty, smelling of alcohol and somewhat shaky, badly in need of a shave, wearing rumpled clothes that looked like they had been slept in for a few days. The man was obviously in a lot of pain. He wasn't familiar to any of us, but he had been to one of Peter's services several months before. During the service, something deep had stirred, and in this time of crisis, he was reaching out to be heard, to be helped. Peter stopped everything and just listened intently. The man was incoherent at times, but the compassionate attentiveness of Peter and his few well-chosen words quieted his troubled spirit and gave him the reassurance he needed.

What struck me even more was the look on Peter's face after the man left. It was ancient, yet timeless, a look of total compassion and heartfelt love. It was expression I was to see often during the years we were together.

With Peter, I had many experiences with Higher Mind and altered states. Peter opened the door to new dimensions of reality for me. A particular experience comes to mind. Peter and I were at a conference in Chicago. Harmon Bro, a popular lecturer and writer on the Edgar Cayce readings, was on the program. During his lecture, he recalled with great feeling the birth of his fourth child. He was in the waiting room at the hospital, all alone, when he started to hear music. But there was no audible sound, no piped-in music. What he was hearing was the music of the spheres, the sounds that accompany the birth of every soul. My heart exploded with that thought. Tears streamed down my face. If prayer is the desire of the heart, then a mighty prayer was uttered that I, too, might one day hear the celestial music.

Little did I know how soon that prayer would be answered. The next evening Peter was the featured speaker. After his talk, Peter lead a healing service. As the audience sang "Alleluia" as an accompanying sound, he invited anyone who wanted healing to come up for the laying on of hands, I felt the urge to go forward. When Peter touched my forehead, it felt as though the top of my head opened and there was an enormous funnel rising up through the heavens. I was lifted into another reality. I was still aware of the faint "Alleluias" in the background. Yet I could hear ethereal music and see indescribable colors from other dimensions.

This "opening up" was one of many experiences with altered states that I had with Peter. There is a subtle danger in a relationship with a "god-man." One needs to always make a clear distinction between the experience and the catalyst. Once that distinction becomes blurred, there is an unhealthy dependence on someone else for your spiritual life, which can keep you from trusting your own inner source.

On the personal level, there were different challenges and paradoxes to be resolved. On the one hand, the experience with Peter and his spiritual organization was rewarding and fulfilling. There were opportunities to teach, learn, and share in a dedicated group with a common goal. The impact of the group was far-reaching, extending into Europe, Africa, and Australia. I thrived on the broad scope of the vision. And it was rewarding to see people's lives being changed. I was kept so busy with the newness of it all, with the travel, teaching, planning, and organizing, all of which I found so stimulating, that my issues with Peter were overlooked.

Unresolved elements of my Dragon Fight were being played out with Peter, and, for much of the time, I was an unconscious participant in the battles. The same qualities I had admired in my father were transferred to Peter. There was an admiration for his knowledge, a yearning for his philosophic understanding, a respect for his authority and strength, and an absolute delight in his humor. The deep feelings I had so naturally felt for my father were transferred to this other wise, strong man. And the same uncanny attunement that I had with my father, knowing words before they were said, sensing feelings even if they weren't expressed, was also a parallel. Both men were my beloved "rabbis."

I respected both men as strong authority figures and with both I reacted against their control. I was special to my father and to Peter. Part of me enjoyed the specialness, and I played it as the Pleasing Passive and Rescue Me Maiden, remaining in the background in a support role, devoted to Peter and his work.

As time went on, I noticed that, with my over-concern for Peter's welfare, his health, and organizational needs, I was losing a sense of my own boundaries. Being *other*-oriented and neglecting self are typical of the co-dependent. I became alerted to my dilemma. Underneath the passivity and mask of niceness, there was hostility.

The anger wasn't directed at Peter, but at myself for being emotionally, mentally, and spiritually co-dependent. Of course, the anger was veiled, just as I had disguised the anger I sometimes felt toward my father, as a child.

Peter was very much the center of his organization, with the rest of the staff playing a supportive role to his leadership. As my work started to expand, it became increasingly difficult to keep a balance between supporting Peter and attending to my own needs. My relationship with Peter shifted. Now, instead of being special, I was subject to harsh criticism.

"You aren't committed to the work. You only want to do your own thing!" would be the recrimination.

I would vacillate, afraid to be on my own, yet wanting to be on my own. As my work developed, I could see it was going in a different direction than Peter's and I couldn't see how the two could merge. If I were going to be a partner, as he suggested, I needed to make a full-time commitment to his work. And though I resonated with much of Peter's vision, there was another stirring in me that could not be quieted. Peter could neither understand nor embrace that stirring, and I would not and could not deny it.

We both vacillated. He was as inconsistent as I. Peter made it clear that he was married to his work. Any relationship beyond the scope of that work was a distraction. On the other hand, there were periods when a strong personal relationship developed, with wonderful moments of tantalizing closeness and intimacy. There was too much fear and not enough trust. I wanted to pull away; I didn't want to pull away. I felt torn. "I want you by my side, I want you as a partner." And then, "A personal relationship interferes with work." He was a perfect mirror for my own indecision. A friend, yes. A teaching partner, yes. A personal partner, no. It was never a real consideration. In fleeting moments it had crossed my mind, but I would readily dismiss the thought as too oblique, not real. The confusion was the fierce loyalty I felt that went beyond anything personal. That wasn't so easily dismissed.

It took me a long time to accept the truth. I wanted out, but I wasn't honest enough or clear enough to choose it. For two years, I had a strong sense that I had learned what I needed from working with the organization. It was time to go. When we ignore inner promptings out of fear and insecurity, we pay a price. Instead of letting go and following my heart's desire, I began questioning and criticizing everything about Peter, his lifestyle, and his organization. The continual changes in the organization, which had always seemed fascinating, now seemed to be an unhealthy vortex of confusion. It was time for me to move in a new direction; but instead of simply choosing to go, I blamed and found fault. It is much more powerful to move toward something. I was choosing to find fault to rationalize my decision to leave. I had gone from blind loyalty to abject criticism, from one side of the pendulum to the other. Nothing is ever resolved when we seek its opposite.

One particular day, I was spending time with a good friend. I was feeling moody and irritable. The mood deepened and my friend tried to help me turn my despondency around. As we talked, something was triggered from deep inside—anger and rage that had been there from childhood. I turned it on my friend, becoming so heated I thought I could have killed him. Fortunately for me, my friend was also a gifted counselor. He immediately shifted modes. He became absolutely unflappable, allowing me to have my space so that I could experience whatever I needed to. He remained steady and supportive throughout, sensitively knowing when to give space and when to be a gentle guide.

"Look, you can trust me," he said. "Whatever feelings you want to express, whatever you need to say, this is the time to do it. Go for it!"

That was all the permission I needed. I felt totally safe. All the dark feelings and emotions I had politely suppressed and denied for so long came pouring out like an uncontrollable torrent. I wailed and sobbed. I grieved and stormed and mercilessly flailed my pillow. I was encouraged to go further.

At first, it was an anger at Peter, and then at my former husband, and finally diffused anger. Then, from the depths of my self, from the very core of my being, a rage and resentment surfaced toward my father. Buried memories and forgotten feelings bubbled up. I recalled the times when he let me down, when he didn't stand up for me, when he denied me the special time I needed. The heartache and the tears seemed endless. I felt helpless and overwhelmed, as though I had tapped into an unending sea of pain. My fear was that I would be trapped, a prisoner with no way out. I reached a moment of deep catharsis. The timing for such a moment can never be planned. Though it can be assisted, it must occur somewhat spontaneously. I knew I could not be forced into my depths, or I would feel the pressure to perform. I had been given the sacred space to be totally one with the experience, to allow it to happen, neither forcing it nor preventing it. There was a subtle moment when I knew that I could stuff it down again as I had in the past, or go even deeper into the experience. I surrendered totally to the moment. More memories, more sobbing, and then, there was a deep release. I felt an overwhelming sense of love and exquisite peace. My father no longer had to be the flawless, faultless paragon of strength and wisdom. He was a human being, with faults and virtues. Now I could love him in a much more profound and mature way. The final remnants of the Dragon Fight were over at last. It was time to say a final farewell to the over-identification with the role of Pleasing Passive. It was time to own a more genuine self.

The catharsis resolved the paradox with Peter. The issue was no longer whether I was for or against Peter and his work. Paradoxes are resolved when we move out of duality. My focus shifted. I was ready to follow my own heart, listen to my own rhythm, and move into a different phase of my life's work and purpose. There was no confusion, no conflict, nothing to fight for or against. It was a natural process, not to be feared or denied, but welcomed and embraced.

Two dreams validated this new direction. In both, I was sitting at a table, face to face with Peter, talking directly and clearly. Peter's beard, which I associated with his public image, was missing. There was no facade, no covering, I could see him as he was. The masks were removed. The fantasies were over. We communicated with openness and directness. I no longer had the need to either adulate or unfairly criticize. He was a beautiful man, a gifted teacher. The dreams indicated I had come into balance with my male side. There would be more freedom in following my inner authority. The paradox had been resolved. I was at peace.

Positive Qualities	Challenging Qualities	Response
Determination Inspiration Awareness Faith Compassion Knowledge	Feeling overvalued/ undervalued Unpredictable emotional swings Shut off feelings	Pleasing Passive Wilting Bitch

Co-Dependency	Gold
Spiritual (knowledge) Emotional (upheaval and uncertainty)	*Get my own inspiration *Take responsibility for own work *Empowered to teach *Knowledge

Coming to Clarity—Francis

In my myth, Peter was the powerful king, and Jason was my shining knight. The king is a man of authority, of truth and understanding. The knight goes in quest of the high ideal. He is romantic and magical, there to fight battles and be a protector. Both the knight and the king enjoyed a fair lady at their side. With both, I played the "Pleasing Passive" all too frequently.

Jason opened my heart, and Peter connected me with a Higher Mind. I was definitely emerging, but the process wasn't complete. I needed to become much more genuine. It was too easy to ignore and cover up what I didn't want to look at or deal with, and to look outside self for acknowledgement and validation.

And the Universe sent Francis.

My first impression of Francis was favorable but not memorable. There was nothing in the original meeting to indicate the important role he was to play in my life. Maybe that was because his background couldn't have been more different than mine. He came from the tough north side of Philadelphia, a world that was totally unknown to me. He had owned a nightclub and had earned his living as a bartender, before dropping out to search his spiritual path.

Francis was an astrologer and counselor. Astrology was something I had never put much stock in. But, at the time, my husband and I had been separated about six months. With all of the changes in my life, I was ready for help, in whatever form it might take.

I made an appointment for a reading. When the time came for the session, Francis greeted me warmly. As we sat down, I felt the penetrating look of his bright hazel eyes, as if he were looking all the way through me to the tip of my toes.

With little introduction, he began his reading. "As a little girl, sometimes you had difficulty understanding your mother," he began.

It wasn't a question, but a statement! I was caught off guard. How could he know something as personal as that! "You were not an easy child. You challenged her. But on the other hand, she imparted her strength of character to you. Do you appreciate it?" he asked.

"Appreciate it," I thought. "I never thought of it like that."

"She's the perfect teacher for you. That's why you chose her. See here," he said, holding up what was obviously my horoscope. You're very feminine, ultra-feminine in the extreme, always yielding, always adapting to your environment. You become the perfect mirror, reflecting back what you think others want from you, especially the men in your life. You can't do that with your mother. She forces you to take a stand, and that's helped you to develop your strength."

His comments rang as clear as a crystal note. I knew what he meant immediately, but I had never thought of it in such a positive way.

"As a child, you were very intuitive. You had many visionary experiences. There were times you knew things before they happened, didn't you?"

I had never told anyone about my childhood experiences. I had always been my secret. A door to my inner self suddenly stood wide open. He had the key. The room was dark and filled with secrets. I didn't know if I wanted to turn on the light to show everything inside, but I knew at least I didn't want to shut the door.

"Your chart shows that now is a transitional time for you," he said. "It's as if there are two different people, an old self whom you are leaving behind and who over-identified with other people's expectations and a new self who will teach and travel, taking you to many different parts of the world. That's your destiny," he said, jarring me with his directness. And then, with what sounded like a tone of warning in his voice, he continued. "But you have to become stronger within yourself. Otherwise you will always be absorbed by whomever you are with and lose your identity."

As he spoke, something seemed to explode inside me. His face began to change, and he became enveloped in a luminous glow. A multitude of images flashed and faded across his face in rapid succession. Perhaps sub-personalities, perhaps former incarnations. I didn't know how to determine what they were.

I had never had an experience like this before. His words seemed to open up new parts of my being. Suddenly, I felt an incredible connection to him that transcended the physical dimension. All of a sudden, I was looking inside his body, as if his flesh had dissolved, exposing his bones, organs, and arteries.

At the same time, I could feel his intense connection with me. It was magnetic and powerful. There was nothing I had experienced before that could give me a frame of reference for these feelings. It was more than I could handle.

I realized that, with such an intense bond established so suddenly, we must have known each other in other lifetimes. Our connection felt too deep and strong for it to have been a first encounter. It was an uncanny feeling. He knew things I never shared with anybody and hardly admitted to myself. I was both fascinated and frightened. On the one hand, I felt an instinctive urge to try to conceal parts of my life I was ready to reveal. I had years of being conditioned to be vague and secretive.

It was as if a part of me was shouting, "This is it. This is what you need. Be open and listen." And at the same time, another part was struggling to protect my ego and resenting the invasion of privacy, fearful of stark reality. I found myself reaching the limits of being open and then stepping beyond, still uncomfortable about not being as open and honest as I could.

This is ridiculous, I thought, after the session ended. Why am I hiding things? Why did I feel it necessary to be covert and couch things in terms that I thought would be acceptable to him?

The next day we met again and took a long walk on the beach. He continued to ask questions. If one answer didn't feel right, he would ask another question, going deeper. No surface response would do. At some level I knew I needed a crash course in opening myself up, and what I attracted was the most challenging relationship of my life. On one level, I wanted to break through my self-imposed ego barriers. So I attracted a man into my life who would insist on openness, confront me at my point of greatest vulnerability, and challenge my values. Our relationship developed quickly. It was intense, passionate, and honest.

There was no way to kid Francis, to tell a half-truth or to make something better than it was. There was no need to "fluff pillows." Francis challenged me to drop the guises, to drop the need to have the "right answers." Just tell the truth. I worked on being open, continually uncovering new barriers and dropping my resistance, experiencing new dimensions of freedom. It was challenging, liberating, and scary. No sooner did I feel I had crossed one threshold than there would be another staring me in the face. I continually found myself reaching the limits of my openness and then allowing myself to move through those awkward moments. When I found that too threatening or more than I could handle, I simply shut down.

There were moments of being able to gently let down the ego barriers to reach a new peak in intimacy, openness, and sharing that was totally new for me. It was a level of loving that I had never experienced before. It established a reference point for what it is like to hide nothing and to be totally accepted. Often though, it took sexuality to reach those depths of intimacy. I could lose myself in Francis for days at a time; we could live in a fantasy world. We could both talk freely about anything and everything. After years of so many suppressed feelings, it was a welcome relief not to have to pretend, to just be natural, and to love and laugh and be.

Nevertheless, Francis was an invaluable guide as I went through the confusion of sorting out my past from the present. We spent hours talking about anything and everything. I was so full of uncertainty about so many things. I relied upon him instead of trusting my own self.

During this time, Peter and Jason were still important to me. Peter encouraged me to teach, and we often traveled and taught together. It was fascinating, fulfilling, stimulating. When I was with him, I was totally absorbed in Peter and his work. When Jason and I were together, I became caught up in our magical togetherness, and Francis would be out of my mind, out of my thoughts—until I was with him again.

Francis was ready for a committed relationship. I wasn't. I still enjoyed Peter and Jason, too. Or so I believed. When Francis confronted me with my vacillation, I would once again become absorbed in him. I was willing to reflect back everything I felt or thought he wanted to see or hear. And it infuriated him.

"How can you love me, and still want to be with other men? You're like a leaf in the wind," he barked. "You don't know where you stand!"

It was impossible to be the Pleasing Passive anymore. I didn't want to acknowledge my inconsistencies, so I became the Icy Maiden—cold, aloof, distant, withdrawn. And the colder I became, the angrier he became. He would explode in volcanic, fiery outbursts that were threatening and confrontational. And while he acted out his rage and resentment, mine stayed inside. He was my shadow, dramatizing the unrecognized anger I couldn't express. It was high drama—wild extremes and blind projections; fire and ice, not love.

Ultimately we reached an impasse. I didn't want to give him up, and I wanted everything else too! And he insisted that I make a choice. Conveniently, I chose to avoid the issue, and he wanted to force it. I would dread seeing him, and then surrender to his magnetism and passion. After our love-making there were still the unresolved questions.

We were tearing each other apart, stuck at our crisis point in the relationship and not able to push through it—and still calling our addicted state, love.

I was relieved when an opportunity came to do a speaking tour with Peter. It was a welcome relief and an escape. For two weeks, I could put Francis behind me; but on the night I returned, the inevitable showdown took place.

I hadn't been back for more than thirty minutes when Francis called me on the phone. We got into an argument. Irritated, I hung up. Next, I heard a loud, insistent knocking on my door. From the window, I could see Francis, and he was angry! I simply didn't want to deal with it, so I ignored the knocking. The knocking became louder.

"Go away," I called through the door. "We'll talk about it tomorrow."

"This can't wait!" he insisted.

I didn't want to deal with the drama and emotion. Francis went around to the back door to see if it had somehow been left open. Finding it locked, he came back around to the front once again and pounded persistently on the door. Again, I ignored the noise.

"Francis, we'll talk about it tomorrow." The resentment in my voice was obvious.

"The hell we will," he bellowed back. Suddenly, as if in a scene from a low-budget film, Francis kicked through the locked door with a resounding crash, tearing the jambs from the wall.

"This is crazy," I thought as he strode over the fallen door. "Who does he think he is!" Suddenly I was overwhelmed by how crass this whole situation was. How did I get into this mess anyway!

"Get out of here!" I shouted as I lunged at him and tried to push him back through the ruptured door. "Get out! I never want to see you again!"

Then, both his hands were on me, gripping me hard. Francis yanked me by the nape of the neck and pulled me into the bedroom, and threw me down on the bed. I was too startled to react. He glared down at me, his eyes flashing with anger, his lips trembling with suppressed force. And then, without saying a single word, he straightened up, turned on his heels, and stormed out the door.

I felt violated, angry, bitter, and relieved it was over.

I didn't hear from Francis for three years. For a long time, I felt very judgmental and superior about what had happened. I was definitely the victim of his rage, or at least that was my interpretation. How convenient it is to externalize blame. That way we prolong and avoid personal responsibility.

In retrospect, that episode was in important metaphor of what was going on inside me. For years I had been conditioned to be vague and secretive; now the door was wrenched open. Francis (or that part of me that was angry about the pretense) was intent on crashing through all my barriers, and I was equally intent trying to protect myself. I wanted to hold on to my self-image. I liked being admired, sought after, and considered spiritual. I wanted to be on my mountain top, seeing dreams and visions, not down in my lowlands, dealing with emotions and facing fears.

The door crashing open, with the chain yanked from the wall and splinters flying, was the shock I needed to wake up and take a hard look at the hidden, murky, shadowy parts of myself.

The Healing Process: The Road to Love

For the next three years I worked on strengthening myself. All my primary relationships with men had come to an abrupt end. My father was dead, I was estranged from my brother James, Jason was married, Francis was gone, and my work with Peter was held to a minimum.

Now, instead of filling up my time with relationships, I spent time with myself, looking within.

I explored the repeating patterns and the negative feminine and got to know all her names: the Icy Maiden, the Queen Bee, the Pleasing Passive, Rescue Me, and many others. By embracing these parts, their power over me was diffused. I had touched my depths; I was ready to soar. I spent time loving and supporting myself and noticing when I would step back into dysfunctional modes and relationships that had upheaval, insecurity, hype, the adrenalin rush, uncertainty, and the emotional co-dependency that had been my biggest challenge. Instead, I was transforming my need for the unhealthy edge, as evidenced in my need for relationships to be exciting and stimulating. I was putting that same energy in the creative edge, where my need for excitement could be fulfilled in a healthy way.

I was becoming much more attuned to habits which still kept me on the dangerous edge and curbing those tendencies much quicker. I would still want to wait until the last minute to pack before trips, see how low the gas tank would get before I would fill it, or forget to pay a bill on time. But the reckless self-sabotaging self was less in charge. I was noticing what I was doing much more quickly now, forgiving myself, and making positive changes. Peace, order, and harmony were becoming the order of the day. There was much more kindness, caring, and acceptance both within and without.

It was an important period. Meanwhile, my work was expanding. The leaf that had been blowing around in so many directions, subject to the variable currents, had discovered that inside there was a seed. That seed had taken root in the earth. There were still leaves blowing in the wind, but these leaves were on branches connected to a trunk, connected to roots. I was finding my place.

During this time, a friend and I decided to do a marathon together. This is a process in which two partners get together for forty-eight hours of uninterrupted time. For the first twenty-four hours, one partner talks, and the other listens. And then for the next twenty-four hours, the roles are reversed. The purpose of the marathon is to create an opportunity to share your life story, while your partner agrees to listen with the heart, offering no commentary, judgment, or criticism. It is a process of profound self-discovery and acceptance.

And so, in the presence of a trusted friend, I found myself sharing all my fears, sorrow, fantasies, joys, and confusion about my life, particularly the transitional period. We laughed and we cried. The bonds of trust between us deepened. Insights had space and time to emerge gently, without force. Memories floated up spontaneously from hidden spaces. Patterns and cycles began weaving together. For the first time, I saw clearly the repeated themes playing out in my life.

At one point, I found myself talking about Francis. As I talked about him, I discovered that my feelings of rage, resentment, and self-righteousness had dissolved. I saw him now in a totally different light. I remember what he had said on that very first day. My challenge was to get strong. If I didn't, I would always be absorbed by whoever or whatever was around me.

"You want to do spiritual work?" he had said. "The most important work you can do is know yourself. Do that and everything else will fall in place."

I knew now exactly why I had attracted him into my life. He was the perfect complement—someone who insisted on honesty, someone with an obsession for clarity, someone who hated pretense and sham. It was what I needed in my life, in my self.

His own explosive anger, his volcanic outbursts simply mirrored what was bottled up and hidden inside me. All during that time, he was trying to get more connected with his femininity to balance and soften his negative male energy. And so he attracted me, someone ultra feminine. On the other hand, I needed to bring out more of my masculinity, more of the authoritarian male energy, to stand up and express my thoughts, feelings, and beliefs with confidence. Francis had come into my life to force me to deal with my emotions and to strengthen what was underdeveloped and weak inside me. He did his job well. We were at opposite ends of the same issue. It was a perfect match. I completed the marathon, knowing that it was a big turning point for me. I was ready to end blame. A few days later I dreamed about Francis, which confirmed my inner change.

In the dream, I walked into a big house. Francis was there. We hugged one another, and, as we embraced, I felt warmth and acceptance.

Almost from the beginning moment of seeing Francis again, I sensed a genuine change. It can be challenging to shift a relationship which has a history. I was sure we had.

As if to challenge this new level of friendship, we were presented with a test. I had been a little on edge for a few days. I happened to run into Francis and he suggested we take a walk on the beach. One the way we started getting into a disagreement.

As the tension mounted, I started to distance myself from Francis, shifting into an old pattern, shutting down and withdrawing. At the same time, I was aware that Francis was trying very hard not to be affected by my mood.

In the past my ice would bring out his fire. All the time I had been withdrawing into my shell, Francis didn't react. There wasn't any anger. There wasn't indifference either. He was genuinely communicating in a supportive way. My mind observed that, but I was too emotionally distant for it to matter.

We got out of the car and walked along the beach silently until we found a spot where we could sit down. It was fall, and the normally crowded beaches were deserted. The only sounds were the rhythmical crashing of the waves and the screech of hungry gulls.

We sat for awhile, looking toward the sea, both absorbed in our own thoughts, our own silence. My anger had become a cold numbness. I was dissatisfied with myself and my inability to feel warm or connected. Where had all the good feelings gone? How does it end?

Gradually I became aware of Francis. He was smiling, and his face was radiant. Our eyes met and it was as if I could feel his heart saying, "I know you're putting out this coldness. . .and there is nothing more to explain, no more insights, no more words, nothing left that I can give. . .and I love you."

At that moment, my coldest, most withdrawn, angry self felt that love. Something shifted inside me. The pain and separation dissolved in an instant, and I experienced an acceptance I had never felt before.

Suddenly, spontaneously, my heart opened. It was a transcendent moment when everything becomes understood. There was just pure love. There was no more struggle. I had merged with Higher Mind. That consciousness was speaking for me and through me. Francis was having a similar experience. He was enveloped by an enormous golden light. It seemed to fill him, and then I felt a transcendent light envelope me. There was such joy. It was indeed a sacred moment.

We both started crying. I had moved into an experience of love that I had never known. We were love expressing itself. The true nature of every woman is love. I had come home to my true self.

Positive Qualities	Challenging Qualities	Response
Openness	Anger	Icy maiden
Integrity	Not rooted	Shrieking
Wisdom	Extremes	war goddess
Understanding	Weak self-image	Seductive
Trust	Critical	siren

Co-Dependency	Gold
Emotional	*Take my own power
(intensity)	*Think for self
Mental (decisions)	*Openness
Spiritual	*Develop my
(self-knowledge)	own philosophy
	*Self-understanding

Exercises

The Forty-Eight-Hour Marathon

The forty-eight-hour marathon is an opportunity to talk openly about yourself and your life to supportive a partner and to be heard by that person without judgment.

1. For forty-eight uninterrupted hours, you and a partner stay together in a room, going out only for restroom breaks.

2. Arrange for food and drinks to be prepared and brought to you in your room if possible, or make meal preparation simple so that your focus is not taken away from your process.

3. Each partner has twenty-four hours to share his/her life experience. You may literally take the first twenty-four hours (with short stops for sleeping or naps as you need them) or divide the time into six or eight hour intervals and then change partners.

4. When you begin, start with your earliest memories. As you go through your life, if incidents and memories start occurring out of sequence, feel free to insert them as they arise. Share your

experiences, the people in your life, hopes, dreams, fears, challenges, fantasies, pain, joy—whatever has been in your history.

5. When you listen to your partner tell his/her story, be supportive. Avoid the tendency to give opinions or tell how it reminds you or relates to something in your life. Remember, it is to be uninterrupted.

Parent Picture Review

Review your Parent Picture and reassess whether your significant-other relationship is the same as, similar to, or the opposite of your parents' pattern.

Your Own Charts

Consider three important partners in your life, whether they be a boss, a friend, committed partner, lover, etc. After meditating on them for a few minutes, fill in the following chart for each of those partners.

Positive Qualities	Challenging Qualities	Response

Co-Dependency	Gold

Once a woman claims ownership
of her own inner authority,
she makes a quantum leap into
the highest octave of the feminine.
Her subtler senses awaken: intuition
insight, and sensitivity to
her own rhythm. She touches that delicate
state of grace and experiences the full
power, potency, and depth of being a woman. Her
laughter and her aliveness well up from deep
within, and she gives birth
her natural child—Joy.

Chapter 10
The Highest Octave of the Feminine

Do You Know Where Bliss Is?

India was where it had begun, where the strangeness first wore off the strange. She had been the starting point of my spiritual journey some seventeen years before. She had given me sacred moments where invisible worlds and tangible worlds come more closely in contact. At times, she is the tired old woman who has had too many children. But unlike no other, she has deep wisdom to impart. It was time to go back home to India to see where I was.

Suddenly, almost magically, a trip to India was arranged.

A small but very special group of women were invited to participate. There was a silent consensus that the focus of this trip was not about seeing what could be seen. Instead, it would be a pilgrimage, an inner journey one takes while participating in an outer event.

One of the goals of Hindu spirituality is the attainment of Bliss, or nirvana. And so it seemed rather significant that on this trip to India, I found myself in a literal search for Bliss. Bliss is the name of a compound in the vast complex of Auroville, a spiritual community in the south of India.

Auroville, inspired by Sri Aurobindo and the Mother, belongs to no one in particular, but to humanity as a whole. In a sense, it is an experiment in global integration, representing contributions from more than 120 countries and possessing a population of over 700 residents. The community stretches over acres of lush, green land, the result of careful reforesting and by-hand planting of every tree on the property. It is composed of many compounds, or districts, each with a distinctive name, such as Bliss, Silence, and Transformation.

One of the women in our group knew the administrative head of the community. We decided to visit her, which seemed a simple enough task. All we had to do was find Bliss, where she happened to live.

Our map clearly indicated the location of Bliss. But, as we approached the entrance to Auroville, we decided to re-check our directions with several East Indians standing nearby, who were quick to oblige.

"Can you tell us the way to Bliss?" we asked.

"Sure, sure," they responded, their heads bobbing from side to side. I had yet to learn that Indian head-bobbing and agreeableness has little to do with whether or not one might actually know the way. It simply means "Sure, I will give you directions," which has no bearing on whether the directions are correct or not.

The directions seemed clear. Down the road two miles, left at the fork in the road, cross the bridge, take the third turn on the left, and the first house on the right will be Bliss!

We followed the directions precisely. All went well, except that after we crossed the bridge and took the appropriate turn, the first house on the right was not Bliss. In fact, there weren't any houses in sight. At the moment of this perplexing revelation, a young man came buzzing down the road in the opposite direction on a motor scooter. We hailed him down and asked once again, "Can you tell us how to get to Bliss?"

He stroked his beard thoughtfully. "Ah, Bliss. Yes. Yes. I have heard of it, but I've never been there." He smiled and began the by-now familiar head bobbing. "But I can tell you, you're going in the wrong direction. It's not west. You must go east." We were given yet another set of instructions.

We turned the car around and headed back the way we had come. For two bumpy miles we followed the road east, turned left at the fork, crossed the bridge, and at the third turn, proceeded left. Except that, when we made the final turn, instead of finding Bliss, we were greeted by an empty field and more exasperation!

Almost as if on cue, a member of the community appeared on the road headed our way. Again the same question: "Do you know how to get to Bliss?"

"Ah, Bliss," she said, as if remembering it fondly. "I have

heard of Bliss, but I have never been there. I do know where it is, though." The drama being played out was beginning to take on surrealistic overtones.

"But you have come the wrong way. The map is incorrect. You don't go either east or west. Instead, you must go north. What you need to do is to go half a mile down this road and turn right. Go about three miles and then you will come to a clearing. Go past the clearing until you come to a small bridge. Cross the bridge and the first house on the right is Bliss."

Finally, we thought, she seems to really know the way. Off we went again, following the directions precisely. And sure enough, just as we crossed over the bridge, there was a house on the right. It was a charming cottage with a beautiful, well-tended garden. Delighted with our discovery, we approached the house and walked under an lush green arbor infused with the scent of jasmine. The smell had a gentle, calming effect and helped diffuse the tensions that had been building. Darkness was beginning to set in, and, as we walked closer to the cottage, there was a warm glow of light visible from the kitchen window. Inside was a young woman with a serene countenance, happily preparing dinner, a perfect metaphor for the inhabitant of a domicile called Bliss! We knocked at the door and the woman appeared, warm and gracious.

"Hello. Is this Bliss?" we asked.

"Oh, no," she said as she stepped from the door. "This is Serenity."

She wiped her hands on her apron and with a broad smile said, "I have never been to Bliss, but I can tell you how to find it."

And for the fourth time, we listened to instructions on how to get to Bliss—different, of course, from the earlier versions. We were told to go in a direction opposite to the one we had taken, this time south.

We piled back into the car and bounced along the rutted road for a short distance. Suddenly Diana, one of the women from our group, started shouting dramatically, "Stop! Stop the car!"

She waved her arms wildly and pointed toward the left to a dirt road, much too narrow for our car. "Bliss is down there. I know it is! I know it is!"

"No, Diana, that's not where the woman said. It can't be down there!"

"I'm sure it's somewhere on that road," she insisted.
Not at all daunted by our contradictory opinions, Diana
opened the car door and bounded down the narrow road, leaping
and dashing like a gazelle, while a chorus of weary women tried
to call her back. She ran for at least a half-mile until she realized
we weren't going to follow. Reluctantly, she returned to the car,
still insisting that she had found the road to Bliss.

By now, there was total darkness. We agreed that the only
sensible thing to do was to give up our search and head back to
the hospitality center. Our fierce determination yielded to our
more immediate needs of hunger and weariness. We were ready
to give up on ever finding Bliss.

When we arrived at the hospitality center, we were immediately directed through the main building to the courtyard. The
tranquil scene in the garden was a welcome relief from our
disappointing day.

Seated by candlelight underneath a beautiful banyan tree were
a group of people enjoying a special moment together. There was
animated conversation and a kind of intimacy that only comes
from heartfelt connections. The tree was enormous, fifteen feet
or so in diameter, with majestic branches that reached up to the
sky and cascaded down into the earth, rooting again and forming
more trunks. There was something primeval about the tree,
something magical and other-worldly.

Could this be Bliss? The scene had many of the qualities we
associate with that word: peace, stillness, beauty, intimacy,
connectedness.

Myriad thoughts ran through my mind. Maybe Bliss didn't
really exist. Or maybe it didn't matter whether it existed or not.
Maybe the journey was all that mattered. And maybe we
wouldn't have recognized it if we had seen it. Maybe the little
old weaver that we had seen patiently sitting at his loom the day
before, where he sits day after day, hour upon hour, still and
serene, was Bliss. He had never sought it. He had consistently
done the simple tasks. He had found the extraordinary in the
ordinary. And in so doing, perhaps he become the Bliss we
sought.

To satisfy our lingering curiosity about the whereabouts of
Bliss, we asked one of the staff members if indeed there was a
Bliss. Sure enough, Diana had been right after all. Hers was the

true voice of intuition, but we had listened to so many other voices that we didn't recognize the still, small voice when it spoke. It had been the perfect parody.

Ownership of Inner Authority

In the beginning of the spiritual journey, there is often the need to rely on others for guidance and direction. "Others" may include parents, mentors, teachers, authority figures, gurus, bosses, therapists, channels, psychics, friends, husbands, mates, pastors, etc. The need to depend on others lasts for varying amounts of time. And the degree of the need may range from occasional help to total dependency. The irony is that if our answers come from an outside source, there are always the lingering questions: Was the answer valid? Was the guidance correct? And yet, for one not to seek help from an outside source when it is needed is foolish; and for one not to accept wisdom, in whatever form it comes, is arrogance.

Usually, growth is similar to a spiral, a gradual movement, winding upward. There are those moments, though, when we take a quantum leap in consciousness. A quantum leap is a noticeable shift in consciousness. Our awareness expands. Our perception changes. We are lifted into a much subtler vibration. There is a sense of certainty about self, a sense of inner knowing, a sense of connectedness to life. We are in touch with the inexhaustible flow of love and strength from our Higher Power, and our hearts are full. This is the highest octave of the feminine. It is a state of Grace.

Though this shift in consciousness can be precipitated in a variety of ways, often the catalyst for the shift is an experience that challenges us to take full command of our inner authority. In those moments, we are required to trust our inner truth and to rise up and say *yes* to life and to the task set before us. It is *the* major initiation of womanhood.

One of the classic stories about a woman facing the unknown and having the courage of her own inner convictions is told in the myth of Psyche. Psyche is given four tasks to perform in order to redeem herself. (Gathering the fleece from the rams and sorting out seeds, two of these tasks, have already been mentioned in earlier chapters.) The fourth challenge is the most difficult. Psyche is required to descend into Hades, the subconscious realm, and face a series of challenges. As women, we cannot soar higher than we are willing to descend. This fourth and final task is withheld until Psyche has gathered the strength from the preceding challenges. With this final task, she is instructed to get the flask of beauty ointment from Persephone and bring it back to Aphrodite. She is also told not to open the flask.

Aphrodite, the oldest of the goddesses, holds an esteemed position of both power and authority on Mt. Olympus. Certainly, Psyche knew that to violate, in any way, the instructions of Aphrodite would have severe consequences. She would lose all that she had worked so hard to regain. Not only that, but she has already passed through strenuous tasks and has almost finished her long process of initiation. Everything is at stake. It would be foolish to jeopardize herself at this point.

At the critical moment, Psyche responds to her own inner promptings and decides to open the flask, despite the warnings. She immediately falls into a deep, dream-like sleep. It would seem that all is lost! Instead, quite unexpectedly, Eros swoops down and lifts her to Mt. Olympus where she is welcomed as a goddess in her own right. She has emerged out of her illusions of limitation and has opened to her goddess power! As a final statement of her newly earned status, she marries Eros, amid the approval of the gods and goddesses of Mt. Olympus. The marriage symbolizes the integration of her femininity and masculinity. From that union, a child is born, appropriately called Joy.

Initiation Into Womanhood

The myth presents some important insights into the archetypal dimensions of a woman's journey. As women, we face more than one turning point in our lives. The moment of initiation into womanhood, or when we claim our goddess power, however, is a singular experience, characterized by a unique set of characteristics. Other experiences may be similar to this major initiation. They may be important steps, significant and strengthening. Unless certain characteristics are present, however, those experiences do not qualify as the major initiation of a woman.

The major initiation is characterized by both right decision and right timing. Most important is that it be a moment when you recognize that there is no authority but your own inner authority. It is indeed a holy moment. Usually, there is no one to support you, either immediately before or during the experience. There is purpose in that requirement. You must stand in your own truth. And you must do it alone. It is as though the angels themselves are held back in waiting. They wait for you to trust the truth of your own innate wisdom.

Psyche followed her own inner voice. It was contradictory to the outer authority. Her decision to open the flash was spontaneous, genuine, and clear. It was done at great risk. She could lose everything. But it was her truth and she followed it. There is nothing more powerful.

The critical choice that we face in our initiation into womanhood may not be as difficult as other choices have been earlier in our lives. In fact, the experience may not be recognized as a quantum leap, except in retrospect. The preparation for this moment has taken years. We are seldom aware of the progress we have been making. When the time comes for the big leap, the strength from the little steps we made over the years is suddenly there to support us. Suddenly, seemingly through no effort, we find ourselves at one with our authentic self. We are able to tap our innate power and wisdom.

Whatever decision we make at this juncture in our journey is never reactionary, never against anyone or anything. There is no thought to retaliate or hurt or undermine or defy. Neither is there room for ambivalence or doubt. It is a decision that comes from the heart. It is a moment of truth. It uplifts, just by its very nature. In that moment, we say yes to life and to the task before us.

There is no "right" response that is true for every woman in this moment. The choice may defy rational mind. It may seem like heresy, be labeled immature, irrational, inappropriate, irresponsible, too responsible, too committed, too emotional, not emotional enough, etc. Reactions may be mixed, and it won't matter. The intent is never to please others. What will matter is that it is "right" for you.

The decisions themselves are highly personal. It may be deciding to adopt a handicapped child, marrying a man ten years your junior, staying in a relationship that everyone advises you to leave, committing to a particular kind of service, leaving a secure job for a lower paying one that is more fulfilling, finally standing up to your mother-in-law and defining boundaries, going back to graduate school at fifty, deciding at thirty never to have children, or deciding at forty to have a baby.

Not only must the answer be right for you, but timing must be right as well. Timing means sensing the right moment, being neither premature nor too hesitant. If the timing is off, then you are not yet sensitive to your own rhythm. More experience is required. Life will present another opportunity for you to cross this important threshold at some later date.

The Highest Octave of the Feminine

Once a woman claims ownership of her inner authority, she makes a quantum leap into the highest octave of the feminine. It doesn't mean that life becomes easy. It does mean, however, that she has crossed a threshold which enables her to enter another vortex of energy. Her subtler senses awaken: intuition, insight, and sensitivity to life.

She becomes acutely aware that all life is speaking to her. Her outer landscape clearly reflects her inner landscape. Life becomes the teacher and brings everything she needs to learn. She becomes conscious of the accurate mirrors that are continually presented through people and events.

When she needs help, she knows she has a strong Source within. She trusts that Source to show her the way. Her heart is more open, and she is able to see choices and available options more clearly. She can change easily and quickly, rather than painfully and slowly. There is so much more depth and breadth to her expression, so much more to feel and to be.

When, as women, we begin to touch that delicate state of grace and experience the full power, potency, and depth of being a woman, the only response is to bow our heads silently and be thankful.

Grace is the highest octave of the feminine. It is that total surrender to our Higher Power, which is in control. We no longer need to depend on anything outside as a source of well-being. Our deep surrender and letting go allow all to be. Our laughter and our aliveness well up from deep within, for we have given birth to our child—Joy.

We become increasingly aware of synchronicity, "meaningful coincidence" as Carl Jung referred to it. These moments reinforce our confidence that our inner self is attuned to something larger and more orderly than our conscious mind knows.

Synchronicity can reinforce our awareness that we are on the right track. Recently when I came back from the tour to India, I called a friend of mine, an author in California. At that moment, he was writing about India. Two weeks later, I called him again on the spur of the moment. This time he had just written a sentence about Virginia Beach!

Sometimes, a series of events will carry one theme. For example, I was recently given a beautiful handcrafted angel and promptly found a special place for it in my home. Two days later a note came in the mail from someone with the words "Thank you for being an angel in my life." I was touched. Two days later, a friend in Holland wrote, "This is your year and an angel points the way." And in another few days, a gift arrived in the mail: It was a book on angels!

At other times, these synchronistic moments prove definitely that God has a sense of humor. Recently, I was leaving Gatwick Airport in London en route back to the States. I had purposely waited to be among the last of the boarding passengers. I presented my boarding card and suddenly turned ashen when I realized I didn't have my pocketbook. The plane was only fifteen minutes away from take-off, and retrieving my lost bag was not the top priority for the airplane agents. My mind raced quickly to where I had been: airline check-in desk, foreign exchange desk, security check. . .ah, yes, security check. It might be there. I dashed back to the gate with great anxiety since all the money which I had earned during the last month was in the bag. There, waiting for me was a smiling, uniformed, airplane official. "Miss Marlow," he said, "did you lose something?" How did he know my name? "Well," he continued, with a twinkle in his eye, "it would take someone with a name like yours to drop your pocketbook, money and all, and to have someone with a name like mine to pick it up." I wondered what my name had to do with it. My eyes suddenly noticed the name tag on his uniform— Marlow. We both chuckled. "I always wondered when I would meet my long-lost rich relative." He was referring to the wad of bills I had rolled up, right-brain fashion, inside the bag. I assured him that unfortunately all of the bills weren't large ones.

Those precious moments of "exquisite coincidence" are saying "You are being looked out for. You are on track." And when we get side-tracked, we are told that too! A friend reported that she backed out of her driveway, as she had done hundreds of times, except that she didn't see the car parked behind her and went smack into it. It was a reminder that she was so focused on her thoughts that she was missing a lot of life around her. That day she noticed the sunset for the first time in many days.

The Ladybug

One of the most beautiful examples of synchronicity occurred during a retreat experience at Virginia Beach with a man, proof that males can also experience the highest octave of the feminine.

The last afternoon of the retreat was spent in silence. Each person could choose to go wherever he or she preferred: on the beach, in the woods, in their room, etc. Everyone was asked to find some object that was a significant symbol, one that spoke to the participant in some very personal way. The object was not to be sought out, but rather allowed to find the participant.

The experience of one particular person was especially profound. Tom walked along the beach and was drawn to an old, beat-up copper penny lying almost hidden in the sand, well-weathered by sun and salt. He leaned down to pick it up, not knowing exactly why, and continued down the beach. As he walked, he noticed a puddle of water in the sand. The ocean water had been captured somehow in this little crevice. In the puddle struggled a tiny ladybug, mustering all her strength to keep from drowning, unable to move up on the sand. A compassionate chord was struck inside Tom. He took out the copper penny, which he had stuffed in his pocket, placed it gently under the little creature, lifted him up carefully, and then put him down on the nearby sand, where the ladybug would have a chance for a new life. At that moment, he thought he heard his name being called, but dismissed the thought as pure imagination.

When Tom came back to the retreat house several hours later, there was a phone message waiting for him. His grandmother, who had been the most important nurturing figure in his life, had died. At the same time Tom was on the beach helping the ladybug cross over the water, his grandmother quit struggling in her pain-racked body and crossed over to another life. There was not a dry eye in the group.

Going Home To See Where You Are

There are some important milestones in every woman's life: marriage, birth of a child, the first job, etc. Some of these moments are filled with joy and excitement; others, by their very nature, carry mixed blessings. Such was the case with an experience I had last summer. At that time, my father had been deceased for several years and my mother, though extremely healthy and vital, was clearly moving on in years. It was decided that the time had come for her to sell the family home and move into a retirement community.

The feeling of saying goodbye forever to the family home was a milestone that I hadn't anticipated. With all my traveling and wanderings, I hadn't been there very much in recent years; but still, it was home and an important anchor. Now, for the first time, it wouldn't be there anymore.

What would that be like? Almost all my formative years had been spent in that large, comfortable, white frame home. Every inch of it was carefully etched in my memory, especially so since I had known only two homes in my growing-up years.

Somehow, I was the one delegated to help sort out the household items and paraphernalia. Sorting out the childhood treasures was a reminder of precious memories: colored wooden blocks carved with letters of the alphabet; Easter baskets, pink bows, and green stuffing still in place, but no longer with a delicious nest of foil-wrapped chocolate eggs; my brother's beloved marbles. What a delight to experience these once again, yet bittersweet all the while.

It was a final farewell to all of it. My feelings were mixed. I was happy about my mother's enthusiasm for her new life, yet I was inwardly reflective at the same time. Sometimes you go home to see where you are. It was that kind of weekend.

To add to the feelings of nostalgia, my family had been invited to a reunion at the little church in Browntown, where my father grew up. Browntown is a tiny community nestled in the foothills of the Blue Ridge Mountains. As a child, the town seemed confined and limiting, and I was only too glad when we didn't have to live there. Now, it seemed tranquil and charming.

The Browntown Church is a white clapboard structure with plush green lawns, right out of a Currier & Ives painting.

My mother, two brothers, my sister-in-law, and I were greeted warmly and seated in the back pew. As we settled into our seats, I had a tingly sensation that happens in my body whenever there is about to be an important scene played out. It is as though I am being told to take particular notice, that the next cosmic drama about to unfold will be staged just for me. My intuition proved correct.

A feeling of peacefulness suffused the little church, and my eye was drawn to the shiny countenances of several in the congregation and then to the radiant face of the visiting minister as he walked to the pulpit.

With sparse white hair and frail, almost bird-like delicateness, the minister appeared to be seventy years or older. But his eyes sparkled and his voice was clear and well-honed from years of homilies and counseling.

"I came with a sermon and a scripture reading all prepared," he announced, "but just this moment the Spirit told me to change the topic and the text." He opened his Bible, and with a well-trained eye and sureness borne of familiarity, he thumbed through the pages until he came to a familiar spot.

The people seemed a little more attentive. A few coughs punctuated the silence. And as he began to read, I was delighted and surprised. The spontaneous guidance of the Spirit had led him to a passage that has always been my favorite: "I have come to give you life that you might have it more abundantly." He formed the words slowly and with devotion, weaving a texture of respect and intimacy into the words of the Master.

When he looked up from the book, his face glowed with contentment and serenity.

"When I was a young boy, I tended sheep for my father. And one day, when I was alone in the hills, an angel appeared to me and told me that my life's work was to be one of service, of sharing Christ's message. Because it was one of the purest moments of my life, I have always tried to follow it."

A surge of energy shot through me. It sounded so familiar. It struck a resonant chord. I reflected on my early childhood memory, of seeing my life as it would unfold. This clear knowing, from the very beginning—how does it happen? What is the mystery behind it?

After the service we shared one of those incredible country meals about which city people can only dream. Table after table was laden with homemade fare, everything delicious and bountiful. When we left, I felt nourished on all levels. Simple people, simple words, simple truth, yet profound.

The ride back to Front Royal was on a windy country road. That day it seemed particularly peaceful and gentle, a perfect reflection of the feelings inside. There was such a beautiful synchronicity in the letting go of the family home and reconnecting, at the same time, with deeper roots to both family and Spirit. The outer symbol could go now, because the inner connection was much stronger. It was from these people, this land, this heritage, that I had my beginnings. And it was here, as well, that there had been that early and powerful connection to Spirit.

I could feel my heart expanding to embrace and hold so much more, not only these early beginnings but all the experiences in my life. How similar we as women are, no matter what our roots, our origins, our experiences. Somewhere along our path, we begin to own and embrace all our parts, those parts we consider beautiful equally with those parts we consider not so beautiful— the Bitches, the Dragon Fights, the betrayals, the hurts, the wounds. Whatever has been our greatest struggle is transformed into our greatest strength. All our experiences begin to hold so much more hope, so much more promise.

For a moment, there was a fleeting image of Krishna, the Hindu counterpart of Christ, dancing on the serpent. I had seen this image several times in India and had never understood what it meant. Of course; it suddenly became clear. We emerge by accepting all that we are.

We dance through, with, and, finally *on* all of it! We dance with an open heart. And we dance with great joy!